Van Morrison:

The Mystic's Music

Van Morrison:

The Mystic's Music

by Howard A. DeWitt

Howard A. DeWitt

Published by: Horizon Books
                P.O. Box 3083
                Fremont, California 94539

ISBN: 0-938840-02-9
Library of Congress Catalog Card Number: 82-084426

Consulting Editors: Dennis Roby and Francine Hartman
Cover Design: Dennis Loren

Design and Typesetting by Heyday Books, Berkeley, Calif.

10   9   8   7   6   5   4   3   2   1

Acknowledgements

This book began as a result of teaching History 41: The History of Rock and Roll Music at Ohlone College. The manuscript has been presented to my classes in one form or another since 1975. There were also many people who contributed ideas, information and suggestions for the manuscript and I wish to thank them for their help.

A number of musicians who played with Van were very helpful. Some requested anonymous interviews and I appreciated their candor during the writing of the book. The most helpful comments by Van's musicians came from Mark Naftalin, Tony Dey and Nathan Rubin. There were also significant insights into his career from roadies, concert promoters and a number of people knowledgeable about Caledonia Productions.

The office of Nick Clainos at Bill Graham Productions answered a couple of important questions and the Warner Brothers West Coast offices in Los Angeles and San Francisco were also helpful in searching out key points of reference.

The photographs were provided by Peter Kanze, Billy Asprodites, Chris Bradford, Tom Summy, Don West, Kenny Wardell, Bruce Nichols, Lee Cotten, Jim McCue, and drawings by Vinita Chhugani.

A number of media and entertainment figures offered valuable insights during the writing of this book. Among them are Paul Vincent, Don West, Billy Vera, and Jeff Stolper.

The cooperation of record collectors and store owners was another important part of my research. Among the most helpful were Rip Lay, Dave Schwartz, Dennis Pytel, Dave Catalnho, Ed Diaz, Craig Texera, Rodney Masuoka, Bill Burkard, Lee Cotten, Grant Gibbs, Larry Catlin, Joe Mendoza, Larry Ray, Bruce A. Nichols, Kevin Hoover, Kelly Hoover, and Jerry McBrayer.

There were a number of academic scholars who helped in the formation of the book. Among them are Professor B. Lee Cooper of Newberry College. Dr. Cooper's pathbreaking book, *Images of American Society in Popular Music: A Guide to Reflective Teaching*, published by Nelson-Hall in 1982, was very helpful in the latter stages of this project. Professor Cooper is a pioneer scholar in analyzing the impact of lyrics and music upon the changing directions of American popular culture and I depended very heavily on his work. Professor Carroll Tuttle of the Ohlone College Music Department was also very helpful in formulating my ideas, and Professor Herb Schott of the Ohlone College Popular Culture Department was a critic who provided a great deal of time and effort in support of this project. Dr. Schott was also helpful in selecting records, research materials and books examining popular culture.

The cover was designed by Dennis Loren. Another important figure was Fred Worth who provided the framework for and ideas for the trivia in the second section of the book. Fred is America's foremost rock trivia expert and a serious scholar in the field of rock and roll history. His help was absolutely indispensable.

John Koenig of *Goldmine* magazine was not directly involved in the project but he provided encouragement and often answered inane questions graciously. John was also an important sounding board for my early ideas on the book.

Sam Marich was another important critic. He listened to my ideas and provided a wealth of information on Van Morrison's career. As my father-in-law and a first generation record collector he also provided me with his vast knowledge of the blues. Sam is an extremely capable and intelligent record authority who has been a collector since the 1930s. Without his help this book could not have been completed.

A number of people in Europe provided important information. Morton Reff of Norway, who is Europe's Chuck Berry specialist, provided both information and encouragement during my work on this book. Like many Europeans, he was diligent and generous in his correspondence. Like many Americans, I was not as diligent, but I could not have completed the book without Morton's support.

My parents, Anthony A. and Howardine S. DeWitt were helpul during the project and my brothers, Dennis and Duane DeWitt were also a source of encouragement. Dennis was particularly helpful as he is a record collector trained by his big brother and has succeeded in becoming a Seattle legend.

My wife, Carolyn, and my children, Melanie Dawn and Darin Dion, were an important source of comfort during this project. Darin tore up as many pages as he could and at 18 months and 38 pounds he is well on his way to becoming a gigantic record collector. Melanie played her Nicolette Larson, Crystal Gayle and Juice Newton records as a reminder that there are other popular musicians. My deepest thanks goes to my family for making this project a joyous one.

A number of people in the music industry helped to stimulate my interest in writing legitimate rock and roll history. Although they were not connected with the project they gave me valuable insight into the business. Among these are Tommy Sands, Malcolm Yelvington, Johnny Tillotson, and Billy Vera.

This project was aided immensely by the advice and counsel of Malcolm Margolin and Francine Hartman. They, along with Karen Slobod, provided a number of excellent suggestions during the course of this project. I appreciate the time and care they took with the manuscript and its production.

Finally, I would like to thank George Ivan Morrison for good music, intelligent lyrics, and determination to maintain a degree of aloofness from the music business. I hope that this honest effort to analyze his work is pleasing to such an admirable artist.

Cover photo of *Van Morrison: The Mystic and His Music, Live, Vol. 1*, a bootleg album issued in 1982. *Photo courtesy Jerald LaTorre, Flying Horses Records, Ltd.*

Van Morrison: The Meaning of His Art

This is not as much a biographical study of Van Morrison as it is a work about his lyrics and music. Yet Van's work and his life are inseparable because he is, as many critics have described him, a "song poet." That is, Van's songs reflect not only his musical creativity but also his tremendous ability to capture the essence of common human experiences and problems. By analyzing the myriad forces which have shaped Van's career, this book will shed light upon both Van the artist and his musical art.

Perhaps the most important thing that can be said about Van is that he is truly unique. His career began in Europe in the 1960s alongside many of the groups that later formed the so-called "British invasion" of the U.S. yet Van always was, and remained, his own man musically. He integrated a variety of styles, with particular emphasis on the blues, into a unique fusion that ultimately transcended any attempts at comparison of his work to that of other British groups.

Van's uniqueness also shows in the audience that he attracts. Unlike the music of Bob Dylan, for example, Van's music has never symbolized the values of an entire youthful generation. Instead Van's art is a personal one which reflects the hopes, aspirations, and frustrations of people intent upon surviving without a traditional job or lifestyle. Van is able to communicate his own sense of freedom to the listener creating a feeling of freedom from society's narrow restrictions.

Van's skill at speaking directly to his listener has been enhanced by his ability to express his own growth in his lyrics. Thus Van's raw, pulsating approach to the "good times" music of the 1960s gave way in the next decade to more mature concerns about marriage, children, and the search for permanent happiness. Because of his unique personal approach, Van never succumbed to the popular counterculture values and mindless "power to the people" slogans of the 1960s. As a result he has been one of the few rock artists of that period who has aged gracefully, continuing to write poignant and thoughtful songs while the social changes of the 1970s dated most other songwriters of his generation. In fact, it was the openness and lack of pretension in Van's music which helped to break important new artistic ground later explored by Bruce Springsteen, Graham Parker and Elvis Costello.

When an artist of Van Morrison's stature emerges, there is a tendency to accept his work without analysis. This trend is made worse when record companies hire smooth-talking flacks who offer instant analysis of record lyrics. This shallow commentary only prompts many listeners to ignore the words. In the case of Van Morrison, this is a crucial mistake because lyrics and music interact in his songs to create "song poems." Van's scope

1

Van recalls his days with Them
in an interview with Ray Carr of
the *New Musical Express*.

is small rather than broad-ranging. He tells small personal vignettes and
examines simple topics. But his intensely personal songwriting skills work
these humble materials into metaphors of human aspiration, pictures of
the hopes and concerns of many generations, not just the young. It is this
ability to infuse his songs with personal meaning that appeals to the le-
gions of Van Morrison fans faced with the day-to-day problems of life.
Van's song poetry provides warm reassurance that life, like his compositions, has beautiful rhythm and meter.

Generally, Van Morrison's lyrics have been ignored by the majority of
the public. There is an erroneous belief among rock historians that a small
cult of followers maintain Van's musical popularity. This is preposterous
as a well-placed source within Warner Brothers suggested that Van's poor-
est selling album grossed $200,000. This is not the type of success associ-
ated with cult figures like Captain Beefheart or Wild Man Fischer. In
reality, Van's music has a broad and general appeal to a generation whose
dreams were formed in the 1960s and modified in the 1970s and 1980s. By
analyzing Van's thematic changes it is possible to reflect on the aspirations
of a popular music culture heading for its middle-aged years. The tremen-

dous creative explosion of punk music in the late 1970s and early 1980s is reminiscent of Janis Joplin, Jimi Hendrix and Jim Morrison bursting upon the rock scene in the mid-1960s. These symbols of American popular culture were devoured in a Fellini-like drama, but a song poet such as Van Morrison has survived the reckless carnage of the counterculture born in the 1960s. Van is a survivor destined to continue painting vivid pictures of the forces shaping people's lives in the 1980s. There were brief periods of inactivity in the mid-1970s but Van has always continued to perform in small clubs. The legendary retirement from 1975 to 1977 was simply a period when Van did not release albums. In his solitude Van has created his art without interference from the corporate types, the groupies and the audiences who demand constant hit records. In the 1970s and early 1980s Van increasingly gravitated to small clubs like San Francisco's Great American Music Hall and the El Rancho in Santa Rosa, California. Although these clubs were not patronized by people hollering for rock and roll music, they provided an intimate environment where Van could directly communicate with his audience.

In a sense Van's lyrics and music offer a microcosmic picture of individual struggle in modern America. Bob Dylan proferred a sharp, often political criticism of recent events. The Beatles developed an exciting new direction to traditional rock and roll music, and The Rolling Stones infused a raw emotion into the rock scene. Van Morrison combined all of these elements with a personal, philosophical touch that reflected the tensions of the last two decades. There is a freshness and a sense of integrity in Van's music which makes it appealing in light of the recent success of faceless commercialized groups like REO Speedwagon and Journey. These groups tend to produce formula rock and roll designed for the Album Oriented Rock (AOR) market.

Van Morrison is such a diverse and unique artist that many people wonder where his songwriting skills began. In a small seventy-plus page sketch entitled *Van Morrison: Reliable Sources*, published by Van's Caledonia Production Company in 1974, the source of his musical inspiration is traced to the ancient land of Caledonia in Scotland. Caledonia was one of the few areas that the Romans did not totally conquer in Great Britain. Van believes that his poetic spirit is inherited from the Caledonians. However, this appears to be only one influence. There is also a strain of the Irish literary tradition within his music. In order to understand his song poetry, it is necessary to examine the influences of Irish cultural tradition.

Van Morrison: The Irish Ballad Singer

The ballad singer is a familiar sight in Irish towns. It was common for the Irish poet to sing a street ballad and then sell the lyric sheets. Generally these songs had a contrived simplicity and they dealt with a wide variety of themes and subjects. Van Morrison's songs fit into the mold of the hard-drinking, rollicking street ballads of the 18th and 19th centuries. The common themes of the Irish street ballad centered around love, relationships and the search for happiness. These subjects have continued to occupy Van Morrison's music in the 1970s and 1980s and they provide a link with a number of Irish poets. Another typical Irish poem during the 18th century was the song verse which was generally a romantic story of how a young man met a beautiful young lady. These themes run through Van's *Common One* and *Beautiful Vision* albums. The song verse was also known as *aisling*, and it vanished from the Irish countryside by the end of the 19th century. The songs continued to be sung and were handed down in Irish folklore and tradition.

Perhaps the best example of how Van Morrison was able to use *aisling* in his songs was demonstrated in the "Maid of Cloghroe" which told of the meeting between a lover and his lady while out walking. "Hungry For Your Love" from the 1978 *Wavelength* album is one excellent example of Van's ability to use the *aisling* technique to make some serious comments about life and love.

Another important Irish tradition is the drinking song. In the early 1970s

Van Morrison: The *aisling* technique and Irish drinking songs influence his art.
Drawing courtesy Vinita Chhugani

Van's music reflected the influence of the Irish pub song. A Van Morrison tune like "Moonshine Whiskey" is a drinking song which suggests a search for happiness as well as a release from the world's mundane problems. Van's *Tupelo Honey* album also takes much of its inspiration from the Irish pub environment. Since the album was a reflection of Irish life it was only natural that Van's music was influenced by other examples of everyday occurences in Irish life. Many Irish writers employed irony as a tool and Van's music often uses this literary device.

It was during the 20th century that Ireland produced some of the most significant artists who had great influence upon Van Morrison's song poetry. Perhaps one of the most important of these was James Joyce who had tremendous affect on many other artists' values. In his rejection of many of the traditional values of Ireland—her land, nationalism, social traditions, and Catholicism—Joyce's work, *Ulysses*, describes all human experiences in the space of one day in Dublin. Van has a similar way with words in his Belfast-inspired songs and he is able to develop visual imagery regarding human experiences in the simplest fashion. Yet Van's songs suggest multiple meanings to virtually all his listeners. It is this rare quality which makes Van's music a significant force in rock literature.

In much of modern Irish literature there is a pendulum swinging between acceptance and rejection of Irish cultural values. An example of this contradiction can be observed when Van fondly recalls his Irish youth in his songs. Yet in many other tunes he totally ignores his Irish heritage. Patrick Kavanagh, a well-known Irish literary figure in the 1950s, suggested that "the Irish thing" did not exist in the world of arts and letters. Many Irish writers called for a new direction and this was the background which led to the emergence of young Van Morrison as a song poet.

By examining Van's early life in Belfast and the influence of his family it is possible to place him within the Irish literary tradition. There is a rebellion and rejection of traditional Irish values which many great writers with blue-collar social class origins have experienced and this pattern is similar in Van's intellectual development. There is also a disdain for the countryside and a strong feeling for urban values which gives way to a return to a rural, rustic setting. When Van left New York and Boston for Woodstock and later Marin County in California, he fulfilled the self-contradictory pattern of many Irish writers. In order to understand the influences of Irish culture we will survey Van's formative years in Belfast.

Van Morrison: The Early Years

On August 31, 1945 George Ivan Morrison was born in Belfast, Ireland. For the next fifteen years he was a typical working-class Irish lad. As Van grew up in the atmosphere of post-World War II Belfast, he was exposed to the gloomy influences of a dreary Irish industrial and commercial city. During his formative years Van displayed little interest in school, but he did excel in math and English. It was this early combination of literature and mathematics which served as the catalyst to his songwriting skills. The habit of writing random thoughts in a small journal was a personal trait developed early on which Van has carried over to the present day. Often these ideas are a rush of words from Van's subconscious, and at other times they are finely crafted tunes ready for the recording studio. "I am an inspirational writer," Van told a San Francisco disc jockey, Paul Vincent. This prophetic quote from the early 1980s is an insightful look at Van's creative processes, and he apparently began using this method as a schoolboy. He would keep his notebook handy for the inspirational moment that might be translated into a song.

Perhaps the most influential factor in Van's early musical direction was the selection of records available in his parents' collection. The Morrison family was strongly influenced by American music. Van's mother, Violet, was a jazz-blues aficionado and his dad, George, listened intently to Leadbelly and numerous other blues artists. The house was always full of a wide variety of jazz, blues and country music. In "T.B. Sheets" Van articulates his debt to the train songs of Jimmie Rodgers and the general influences of a number of blues artists. There were also important country roots to Van's music. The "Cattle Call" and "Texarkana Baby" were early favorites of the Morrisons. But these Eddy Arnold songs were supplanted by tunes by Big Bill Campbell and Tex Morton. In addition, the music of Muddy Waters, Sonny Terry and Brownie McGhee and Little Walter helped to shape young Van's early musical direction. The influence of American music and the lure of a new lifestyle prompted the Morrison family to consider a permanent move to the United States.

In 1950 Van's father went to Detroit to visit relatives and for a fleeting moment contemplated moving to Michigan. A number of close relatives lived in Toronto and George Morrison also considered transplanting his family to Canada. Due to the uncertain economic circumstances the Morrisons remained in Ireland. "My family was supposed to move to America when I was five," Van recalls. "Things didn't work out for the move, but all the kids I grew up with thought they were American anyway. See Belfast is not like England..." Van suggested that American influences were much

Van performing at the Old Waldorf in San
Francisco in 1978. *Photo courtesy Don West*

stronger than English ones.

Van was unhappy about the religious strife in his country. He found it
difficult to understand the harsh feelings between Catholics and Protes-
tants, and like many Irish intellectuals he retreated from the confrontation
mentality of many of his peers. Van's interests centered exclusively around
his fervent desire to create music.

By the late 1950s Van was musically educated beyond his years. The Belfast music scene was developing and Van began to attract the attention of
other young performers. As a result, his guitar, harmonica and saxophone
were sought after by a number of musicians. He joined a group known as
Deanie Sands and the Javelins. This folk-blues group covered Kingston
Trio records and played a wide variety of music by other artists. They were
not sufficiently grounded in musical education to consider playing original
tunes, but this gave young Van performing experience. From 1957 to 1959
the Belfast coffee houses offered small audiences who were eager to hear
local artists. There was a rock and roll revolution simmering in these dark
and smoky coffee houses and artists like Van Morrison were learning their
craft and honing their music for a more prosperous time.

One of the ironies of Van Morrison's career is that he is identified with
the music of the first English invasion of America. Van's group, Them, was
considered a minor league version of The Rolling Stones or The Animals.
However, nothing could be further from the truth. Not only was Them not
an English group, but their music was generally more innovative and
complex. On many of Them's early records, Van's lead vocals sound a bit
like Mick Jagger's or Eric Burdon's. But it is impossible to know for certain
whether Van was influenced by The Rolling Stones and The Animals or

whether Jagger or Burdon had seen Van in concert and simply mimicked him. But some evidence suggests that Van may have been the original the others copied. Van's mother told a San Jose disc jockey that Mick Jagger spent an inordinate amount of time listening to Them in the early English pub days and that The Rolling Stones lead vocalist usurped young Van's style. For years the mention of Jagger's name raised Van's anger to a fever point.

It is impossible to know for sure about Mick borrowing from Van, but it is at least clear that Van's musical tastes were more diverse than those of the Jagger or Burdon stylings. An example of this sophistication was Van's attraction to the McPeakes, a traditional Irish folk group. The McPeakes drew a scholarly crowd of young music lovers who blended folk songs with traditional blues tunes. Van met these people in the small coffee houses around Belfast and began the process of integrating their work into his own music along with a variety of other influences as well.

In 1960 Van left school and joined a touring band, The Monarchs. Soon Van was singing other people's hits and some blues tunes to bored G.I.s stationed in Germany and England. In addition to the armed forces bases, The Monarchs played clubs like the Odeon Keller in Heidelberg and the Storyville Clubs in Frankfurt and Cologne. This gave Van a strong grounding in a number of different types of music, as well as an enormous amount of performing experience. As he drifted around England and Europe, Van sketched his future songs in a small notebook.

There was a solitude and frustration to rock and roll music in the early 1960s. As Greil Marcus has suggested, rock and roll music was a "waiting game" in pre-Beatles America. Not only did Van Morrison experience a high degree of hostility over club owners who required matching suits, short haircuts and tightly structured musical sets, many other musicians shared the same frustrations. Each week John Fogerty and The Golliwogs traveled from San Francisco to San Jose to meet Peter Wheat and The Breadmen in battles of the bands. Already Fogerty was scrawling his musical fantasies which later enabled his band, Creedence Clearwater Revival, to become one of America's most popular and creative rock bands in the late 1960s. In Seattle Don Stevenson and Jerry Miller joined the Frantics and learned to play "Fogcutter" and "Werewolf" in nondescript Seattle taverns with groups like Little Bill and The Bluenotes. Stevenson and Miller had a free form view of rock and roll music and they soon began to play the type of music which led them to success with Moby Grape. At San Francisco's Fillmore West Auditorium the Moby Grape carried their music to a new audience and they enjoyed creative, if not financial, success. The Beatles were already well established in Germany and Liverpool but they could not compete with 1960 name acts like Frankie Avalon, Fabian, Bobby Vee and Bobby Darin. It was not a positive time for American rock and roll music. Yet, in this atmosphere, the musical revolution of the mid-1960s was developing in a number of small clubs throughout the world. It took The Beatles' triumphant 1964 American tour to change the direction of rock music.

While Van played in Germany he envisioned himself writing "Miles Davis music," and this hope led to a small part in a German movie entitled *Glide*. Van played the role of a jazz musician and authoritatively carried his saxophone through the movie. It was a non-singing role but one which sparked an interest in writing a soundtrack for a movie. (Van has had a number of his tunes featured in films but has not yet scored a film.) During his years in Germany Van hated wearing the suits required to play in the clubs and he increasingly turned to blues tunes as a performing venue. It was in Germany that Van cut his first single with The Monarchs. "Twingy Baby" backed with "Boozoo Hully Gully" was the first record that featured Van with saxophone accompaniment. It was an inauspicious debut which gave no indication of Van's future musical greatness.

Although The Monarchs were a cover band playing the day's hits, nevertheless Van was an important influence upon the group. He convinced the band to include numbers featuring the music of Jimmy Reed, John Lee Hooker, Sonny Boy Williamson, Little Walter, Memphis Slim and Champion Jack Dupree. This created new musical directions for the band and an inordinate amount of discord. As a result Van returned to Belfast in late 1962.

While in Belfast Van began to form another group from the remnants of The Monarchs. In order to find a place to play, Van approached the Maritime Hotel and soon "Them" was playing in the Rhythm and Blues Club in the hotel's lounge. Them was a typical pub band but they were different from most other Irish rock groups because they performed Van's original songs as well as cover versions of other people's music.

In 1963 Van Morrison and Them moved to London in hopes of garnering a recording contract. They became part of the pub band scene and Van recalls sleeping in the park when money was scarce. When Rice Miller toured England in 1963 under the stage name Sonny Boy Williamson, as part of the American Folk Blues Festival tour, Van was in the audience. Memphis Slim played piano on this tour and such English groups as The Rolling Stones, The Yardbirds, and The Animals played behind the American blues artists. In 1963 the beat clubs were popular hangouts for young English rock and rollers and Sonny Boy Williamson played a number of these clubs. Little Walter was also part of the American blues invasion, and Van found himself in the same hotel with the Chicago harmonica virtuoso. Van would go out for Chinese food and Little Walter would teach Van a few licks on the harmonica. No one realized how important Little Walter's influence was at the time because it steered Van's music away from the pop overtones which meant immediate success. From the beginning Van's lead vocals were influenced by blues shouters, which resulted in a unique and personal blend of rock and roll music.

In 1963-1964 another important change came over Van's music. He was attracted to the Chess Records label out of Chicago and soon songs by Bo Diddley and Chuck Berry were added to Van's personal repertoire. This influence was a significant one because it helped to form the rock and roll songwriting talents which would dominate Van's music from 1969 to 1973. While Van is not necessarily a rock and roll musician, much of his songwriting during the early years had a rock and roll format.

In a 1970 *Rolling Stone* interview Van recalled his formative days and suggested that "I'd go as far as to say that that's how I got into the business, that's how I got there, with Leadbelly and Woody Guthrie and Jelly Roll Morton and Ray Charles. That's what got me started singing." What Van failed to point out was that had it not been for the ferment of the English pub-band days in the early 1960s and the tours through England and Germany with The Monarchs, his music might not have been as diverse and exciting.

By early 1964 Them was almost a year old and ready to attempt to secure a recording contract. The period from 1964 to 1966 was a significant one in Van's career as Them became part of the English invasion of the American musical scene. It was a time of education, frustration and development for Van Morrisón and Them.

Van Morrison: Them, 1964-1966

When Them first began playing in British pubs they were dubbed Ulster's version of The Rolling Stones. Van hated this type of publicity and he stated that Them was an Irish pub band. "The way I like to put it is that Them lived and died as a group on the stage of the Maritime Hotel in Belfast," Van remembered. Initially, the members of Them were Van on vocals, Billy Harrison on guitar, Alan Henderson on bass, Ronnie Millings on drums and Eric Wicksen on piano. They were a raw, emotional, musical congregation who took their inspiration from rhythm and blues, country, folk and traditional blues tunes. For almost six months Decca Records scouted Them and listened intently to the crowds' reactions to Van's vocals. English Decca was uncertain about the musical craftsmanship of Van's sidemen, however, and as a result the company was determined to record with studio musicians.

On September 4, 1964 Them recorded their first song, Slim Harpo's blues tune, "Don't Start Crying Now." The rise of Beatlemania convinced Decca to pursue Them's recording contract and they began to publicize Them as the Irish Rolling Stones. Them's frenzied rendition of this song was augmented by Jimmy Page's exceptional guitar work and a group of

English studio musicians who were able to make the Slim Harpo song strongly rock oriented. In Ireland "Don't Start Crying Now" was an immense hit but it was not until the follow-up record, Big Joe Williams' blues classic, "Baby Please Don't Go," that Them hit the British charts. The cover of "Baby Please Don't Go" earned Them a number eight song on the U.K. national pop charts in January, 1965. This hit was followed by incessant touring, inept management and Decca Records' promotion of Them as young, scruffy rebels. After half a decade as a professional musician, Van experienced a type of success which appeared to be a living hell. The constant touring, broken promises and tension-filled nights in small clubs took its toll on the group. The musicians began openly fighting with one an-

London Records release, *The Story of Them*, an excellent package of obscure Them songs. *Photo reprinted under license from London Records, a division of Polygram Classics, Inc.*

other, often on stage, and in 1965 Them broke up. The problem was that they still had a contract with Decca Records.

"Around 1965 we all decided to split it up," Van remembered. Due to contractual obligations with Decca Records Van and Alan Henderson, the bass player, were forced to record a second album for Decca. Van was willing to work on another album because the first Decca release, *The Angry Young Them*, was a beautifully conceived album with a striking color cover photo. It was also distributed with two different covers in America. When the album was initially released it was entitled *Them* featuring the hit song "Here Comes The Night." When "Gloria" became a U.S. chart song, Parrot Records rereleased the first Them album featuring "Gloria." When Them went into the studio to record the second album there were already rifts in the group. As a result drummer Jackie McAuley, a London art student, and organist Peter Bardens joined the group. Later Bardens became a member of Camel, but here he added an exciting organ sound which complemented Van's lyrics.

Suddenly there were legal problems in the midst of recording Them's first album. The former drummer and piano player, Ronnie Millings and Eric Wicksen, copyrighted the name "Them" and began legal proceedings to use the band's name exclusively. This led to a series of lengthy court battles which hastened the demise of Them. Despite all these problems Them had astounding success since the popular British television show, *Ready Steady Go*, had picked "Baby Please Don't Go" as its theme song. The addition of Jackie McAuley on drums was an important change during Them's first recordings. As the band's first replacement member, McAuley added musical virtuosity because he could also play a number of other instruments.

In November, 1964 Them appeared on *Ready Steady Go* and this appearance on television was responsible for the large number of small concert dates by Them throughout the United Kingdom in 1965. But Them was not a popular touring group as their music was too blues oriented and the English promoters often featured a family variety act to appeal to a wide audience. The days of the astute rock and roll promoter were a few years away, and Van and other English groups suffered from a generation gap in the booking and management of rock acts.

While in London, Van and Them were noticed by a New York record producer, Bert Berns. As a writer and producer, Berns had been successful with black singers such as Solomon Burke, Barbara Lewis, and Freddy Scott. Berns as a songwriter had such classics as "Twist And Shout," "Cry Baby," "A Little Bit Of Soap," and "Tell Him" to his credit. A number of white acts such as the McCoys and Neil Diamond began under Berns' production aegis. In Van Morrison, Berns found a white boy who could sing the blues. When Sam Phillips found Elvis Presley in his Sun Record Company studios, he had much the same feeling that Berns had in 1964. The

New York based promoter realized that Van had an enormous talent which was being held back by the restrictions of the British recording industry. After his first recording session with Van, Berns vowed to lure him to the United States.

In 1965 Them gained some American recognition when three songs from the first album received enough airplay to persuade Parrot Records to issue the group's album with two different covers. What London Decca and the American based Parrot Record Company failed to realize was that Van Morrison and Them were attracting a great deal of attention from rock and roll musical enthusiasts. As Dave Mason suggested during his formative period with Traffic, Van was an excellent performer: "I saw him live several times and, man, he was crazy. He would jump up and down and leap on top of the speaker cabinets." Dave Mason also suggested that Van was highly aggressive and he was able to communicate easily with his audience.

The first year of English stardom was a difficult time for Van Morrison and Them. This was due to Decca Records insisting that Them tour constantly to support their current record releases. From 1964 to early 1966 English Decca released nine 45s by Them, and the recordings combined with personal appearances and touring made the group's life extremely pressured. There were also a number of violent arguments with English Decca over Van's lack of creative controls during the recording sessions. Looking back on the hectic events during 1965 Van remembered "that we were never the same group after we left the Maritime Hotel Rhythm and Blues Club." Van also complained about a lack of money and a general corporate disregard for his artistic concerns.

In 1965 when Them's first album was released Bert Berns was able to convince Van to continue to tour and record for Decca. Since Berns helped to produce some of the cuts on Them's first two Decca albums, he recognized the extraordinary talent of Van Morrison. "Bert Berns was the only guy who had any conception of what we were trying to do, but unfortunately he only produced a few things with us," Van recalled. On Them's first album Berns wrote and produced "Here Comes The Night" and "Go On Home Baby."

Them's first album present something of a quandary for English Decca. The five singles released from the album had some interesting patterns of success. "Baby Please Don't Go," for example, reached number five on the English charts, number two on the Irish charts but only number 108 on the American *Billboard* listings. "One More Time" was number four in England and number one in Ireland and was not released in the United States. "Here Comes The Night" reached number two in England and number 24 in America. "Mystic Eyes" was number 33 in the States but failed to reach the English charts. "Gloria" which was generally acknowledged as Van's most popular early concert song with Them only reached number 71 on the

Van in concert at the Circle Star Theater, San Carlos, California in 1973.
Photo courtesy Chris Bradford

American *Billboard* charts, but the Chicago-based Shadows of Knight had a top 10 hit with Van's song. In Holland "Gloria" was a number one chart song four different times. In terms of English record sales, Them's first album was the eighth best selling album of 1965 and the best selling album on the Irish charts. In the United States the initial Them album only reached the 54th position on the *Billboard* album charts. It was intriguing though that the album remained on the American charts for 23 weeks.

To capitalize on Them's popularity a second album entitled *Them Again* was hastily released in 1966. It was a piece of work which contained only four original songs by Van Morrison but had seven classic blues numbers like Bobby Blue Bland's "Turn On Your Lovelight" and an interesting version of Bob Dylan's "It's All Over Now Baby Blue." In 1970 English Decca repackaged the first two Them albums as *The World Of Them* because they believed that Van's success with Warner Brothers would be short-lived. They failed to package the album attractively and did little to promote this collection of early Them songs.

The two albums that Van Morrison and Them recorded for Decca Records in England were eventually released in the United States by the

London Records subsidiary label Parrot Records. The first English album entitled *The Angry Young Them* had 14 tracks and the second album, *Them Again*, contained 16 songs. In the United States these albums were each reduced to 12 songs. In 1965 the first Them album was poorly distributed and inadequately promoted, and in 1966 *Them Again* quickly found its way into the bargain bins. Despite some incredibly sophisticated blues and rock music, Them made only a limited impression in the United States. Neither album sold well although there was a considerable amount of interest in Van Morrison's vocal stylings. It is intriguing at this stage of his career that Van did not demonstrate any of the legendary shyness or the alleged communication problems which have later prompted a number of interviewers to complain about his lack of cooperation.

In 1966, in fact, Van was generally described as an easy interview by members of the American rock press. There is little doubt, however, that Van's subsequent exposure to some rock journalists precipitated a number of ugly confrontations. Rock and roll journalism during this period was in an infantile state. The teen magazines had no concept of the blues roots behind Van's music, and he was frequently asked inane questions about his favorite color, what he ate for breakfast and who he hoped to meet in Hollywood. To ease the pain of these interviews Van frequently evaded the questions. Yet he always remained a gentleman and in control of himself. Later, he seemed to realize that withdrawal and aloofness were the only effective means of avoiding the rock press.

Even the intelligent rock interviewers like Dick Clark were unable to penetrate Van's newly developed hostility to the slick, business side of the rock music industry. In May, 1966 when Van was interviewed by American Bandstand's Saturday show from Los Angeles, he made it very clear to Dick Clark that his questions were mundane. There was little doubt that Van was not interested in promoting his records through shows like American Bandstand. In many respects Van's difficulties on the American Bandstand Show reflected his problems with Decca Records. Van was expected to do whatever English Decca and American-based Parrot Records demanded. This led to a number of lengthy disputes between Van and Decca.

A good example of the problems in Van's association with Decca Records was the use of studio musicians. Decca executives believed that the musicians in Them could not provide the musical craftsmanship necessary to turn out a suitable commercial album. As a result Decca employed studio musicians on both Them albums. In many respects this was a shrewd move since Jimmy Page was tapped for the studio work and his guitar solos are an important ingredient in Them's early records. But Van and the other members of Them were greatly frustrated by their inability to control either the musicians on the albums or the publicity.

Despite these controversies Van Morrison was carefully developing his songwriting skills. Bert Berns continually urged Van to find models for his songs. As a result, in March, 1965 Van picked up a copy of Bob Dylan's album *Bringing It All Back Home*. Van played it incessantly because one song had a unique fascination for him. In small clubs and obscure pubs Van began performing "It's All Over Now Baby Blue" as part of his repertoire. In Dylan's music Van found the perfect blend of folk, blues, and rock music in an electric setting. When Dylan toured England in 1965 Van Morrison was quietly observing the changing music revolution as America's folk-rock poet was received by an adoring British public. Eventually Van recorded a three minute, 28 second version of "It's All Over Now Baby Blue" which remains one of the most original interpretations of a Dylan song.

In March, 1965 Them was firmly established as an English rock group that had a strong future. But the different levels of chart success in Ireland, Holland, England and the United States only served to confuse Decca executives. They had no idea how to package or publicize this renegade Irish rock group. The unsuccessful attempts to compare Van Morrison and Them to The Animals and The Rolling Stones continued to irritate the group. "They were inventing these images, and they were calling us a British rock group," Van later remarked. Despite three songs on the American *Billboard* charts, and hit records in other countries, Them was a dissatisfied group.

In retrospect, 1965 was an important year for Them. They achieved a degree of rock and roll musical success which assured that they could continue to record for Decca. But as 1965 ended Van Morrison and Them were constantly arguing over their musical direction, the continual touring and their inability to record the type of songs which were suitable for the group. Decca had flooded the 45 record market with five single releases, and there was a strong demand for "Gloria" throughout the world. The success of the Shadows of Knight's version of "Gloria" led to an American tour for Them in 1966. It was a major turning point for Van Morrison because it offered a chance to experiment with his music before an entirely new audience. Like every English rock group in the mid-1960s, Van and Them dreamed of achieving success in America.

When they embarked on their first American tour in the spring of 1966, the rock and roll world was not sufficiently prosperous to support limousines and first class hotels. What Van and the other members of Them found instead were long bus rides, dirty hotels and small amounts of money for food and the simple necessities of life. In addition, many of the audiences in the clubs and halls that Them were booked to play were not familiar with the blues-oriented music of Van Morrison and this led to small crowds and very little money. Once Them came to the West Coast however, things were different. In California, for example, there were ecstatic press reviews and packed houses. In Los Angeles and San Francisco Them quickly became as popular as the Doors or the Jefferson Airplane but this acceptance did not generate increased record sales.

There were some important influences upon Van during his first American tour. Perhaps the most intriguing aspects of the tour for Van were found in the Los Angeles and San Francisco areas. When Them was booked to appear on American Bandstand, Ronnie Harran, the talent agent for the Whiskey A Go Go, was able to sign Them for a 17 night stint in the famed Los Angeles club. Harran, who acted as the American publicist for Donovan, had a particularly keen ear for trend-setting rock and roll music. She had convinced the Whiskey A Go Go to hire Jim Morrison and The Doors as the club's opening act. Phil Tanzini, one of the Whiskey's owners, fired the Doors each week because of Jim Morrison's language and general behavior. However, when fifty girls called the club each night asking about The Doors' performance, Tanzini always quickly rehired them.

Not only was a revolution in American music taking place on the West Coast, the entire rock culture phenomena was giving way to new trends. The Whiskey A Go Go featured such acts as The Animals, the Paul Butterfield Blues Band, the Buffalo Springfield, Captain Beefheart and His Magic Band, and Frank Zappa's Mothers of Invention. Down the street at P.J.'s, Johnny Rivers was carrying on Trini Lopez's legacy by playing to crowds of suits, white shirts and ties, and wing-tip shoes. At the Whiskey however, a

I WON'T COME OUT,
YOU MUST COME IN WHERE
I CONSTRUCT A WORLD
THAT RIVALS THE REAL.
JIM

Jim Morrison of the Doors. Van and Jim sang at the Whiskey A Go Go together in 1966. *Drawing courtesy Vinita Chhugani*

63 year old sculptor named Vito brought in twenty to thirty people a night to dance. Vito had owned a sculptor's studio at 303 North Laurel and in 1966 he attracted a group of young people to his house. Many Los Angeles rock pioneers credit Vito with inventing the psychedelic crash pad, and he was an impressive sight with his bald head and physically fit young body. As Vito and the "Freaks" danced around the Whiskey A Go Go's floor, they began a cultural revolution. No longer were suits and ties part of the rock sub-culture. Long hair, wild-colored clothes and a general lack of concern for traditional manners and morals made Los Angeles an important catalyst in changing the values of the rock music world.

Frank Zappa and the Mothers of Invention immortalized Vito and the Freaks in the song "Hungry Freaks Daddy." In fact, the first Mothers of Invention album contained a tribute to Emperor Vito and Carl Franzoni, who was the legendary young leader of Vito's group. The Mothers' *Freak Out* album was an excellent historical document of the developing musical revolution in California. Although The Byrds, Bob Dylan and rising folk acts like the Buffalo Springfield dominated the American music scene, the popularity of blues-oriented bands was, nonetheless, beginning to make its mark in rock music. Furthermore, the psychedelic revolution also led to the opening of clubs and concert halls which featured dance floors. In San Francisco the Avalon and Fillmore ballrooms attracted large crowds and Chet Helms, who ran the Avalon, even frequently let in young people who did not have the two dollar door charge. Bill Graham presented two or three quality acts at the Fillmore for $3.50. It was the golden age of inexpensive concert entertainment, a free form musical world that Van Morrison and Them fit beautifully.

In May, 1966 when Them played their engagement at the Whiskey A Go Go, The Doors were the opening act. This resulted in a number of nights in which the Whiskey's patrons were treated to Van and Jim Morrison jamming on stage in lengthy versions of Doors' songs such as "When The Music Is Over" or Them tunes like "Gloria." It was an incongruous sight as bikini-clad dancing girls gyrated in little "go-go cages" on each side of the stage and Van and Jim gyrated on stage. In addition to the Whiskey A Go Go, clubs like The Trip, Ciro's, and The London Fog catered to the burgeoning demand for rock and roll. Although The Byrds were Los Angeles' most successful commercial rock group, the direction of American rock and roll music was moving toward the blues and frenetic instrumental and vocal versions of original compositions. When The Byrds began to attract attention at Ciro's in Los Angeles they were considered innovative and revolutionary but by early 1966 The Doors, The Mothers of Invention, and Country Joe and the Fish brought even newer musical and lyrical ideas to rock and roll. And by May, 1966 Roger McGuinn of The Byrds quietly sat in the back of the Whiskey and watched Van and Jim Morrison carry the music into an even more artistic direction.

The fascination with Van Morrison and Them at the Whiskey A Go Go was due completely to their music. Unlike other English rock groups who made mod long hair styles and impeccably styled Carnaby Street suits their trademark, Them simply emphasized the blues. They were a scruffy bunch with an energetic lead singer who refused to compromise his feeling for American blues music. Along Sunset Strip the streets were filled with talk of Van Morrison's performance. Soon Harry Vestine, who went on to Canned Heat, Jim Guercio, who produced Chicago, Mac Rebennack (Dr. John), Grace Slick of the Jefferson Airplane, and Kim Fowley gravitated to the Whiskey to see this outrageous new British act. The lines were long outside of the club for three weeks as Them and The Doors filled it with a type of music that Los Angeles had not previous witnessed.

As a result of these musical changes, recording executives began to visit the club. The Beach Boys' producer, Nick Venet, listened to Them; Lou Adler, who was promoting the Mamas and Papas, watched Van Morrison intently; and a young Warner Brothers executive named Joe Smith quietly took notes on Van Morrison's stage antics. Soon Warner Brothers, at Smith's urging, began a campaign to lure Van to their label. As Van related to an interviewer, "Warner Brothers talked to me for a couple of years, before I signed a contract with them."

Van Morrison as the lead singer of Them. *Drawing courtesy Vinita Chhugani*

In sum, the Los Angeles trip was an important one for Van Morrison and Them. They were discovered by the industry and fellow musicians. In addition, the new directions in American music helped to lift Van's spirits. He suddenly found people like himself, and he was particularly fascinated by Frank Zappa's Mothers of Invention. In the late 1970s Van would add his vocal talents to a Zappa song entitled "Dead Girls of London," thus continuing the friendship that they had developed in the mid-1960s. However, "Dead Girls of London," which was originally intended for an *L. Shankar* album, was never released because Van and Frank could not get Warner Brothers' permission to use the vocal tracks. Prior to requesting permission, Frank Zappa had toured with a huge banner reading: WARNER BROTHERS SUCKS. Frank was suing Warner Brothers to gain a release from his recording contract. Needless to say, Warner Brothers had the last word and "Dead Girls of London" remains an underground collectors' record.

Once the 17 day stint at the Whiskey A Go Go ended, Them traveled to San Francisco to play Bill Graham's Fillmore Auditorium. The opening act was a Bay Area favorite, The New Tweedy Brothers, and when Van Morrison and Them took the small stage there were shouts for "Mystic Eyes," "Gloria," and "Here Comes The Night." San Francisco fans were very familiar with Them's music and danced and applauded the entire night. After the first San Francisco show, Van had a very warm feeling for the Bay Area. The following month on July 29-30, 1966, Them played the Fillmore with Marin County's Sons of Champlin. It was a show where the crowd was predominantly there to see the Sons of Champlin perform, but by the end of the night Them had played three encores and Van Morrison had found another new audience. There were no future appearances for Van and Them in San Francisco, and Van did not bring his solo act to the Fillmore until the spring of 1970. But the San Francisco area had made a profound impact on young Van. He spent a great deal of time in Mill Valley, a small Marin County community, and he began to think of moving there. In the early 1970s Van finally settled into this area as a result of the positive feelings for the San Francisco area that had developed on Them's U.S. tour. It was also a logical move because his future wife, Janet Planet, had grown up in San Rafael, in eastern Marin County.

After reflecting on the first American tour, Van decided to disband Them and return to England. Although Alan Henderson continued to record the group after the 1966 American tour, Them was no longer a successful band without Van's lead vocals. Van was so disillusioned with the rock music world that he momentarily considered changing career directions. But the music was an integral part of Van's personality, and the 1966 American tour was an important one because he met people with similar musical interests.

It is difficult to summarize Van Morrison's brief career with Them. Many of the recordings for Decca Records were excellent, but Van's best work was never released on the Decca albums. Such dynamic musical master-pieces as "The Story of Them, Parts 1 & 2," "Philosophy," and "Friday's Child" demonstrate an unusually creative songwriting skill. Nonetheless, Decca Records in the United Kingdom and Parrot Records in the United States refused to package and promote these songs. In addition, Van's cover versions of blues tunes like "Stormy Monday," "I Put A Spell On You," and "Bright Lights, Big City," generated highly favorable reviews on fledgling FM radio stations like San Francisco's KSAN. Yet there was no attempt to promote Van's blues recordings. There is little doubt that this was part of the reason that Van left Them and returned to Belfast to ponder his future.

Van Morrison: The Bang Years, 1967-1968

In March, 1967, Bert Berns of Bang/Shout Records approached Van Morrison with an offer to join his fledgling company as a solo artist. Van Morrison had originally met Berns when he recorded for English Decca. This was a significant turning point in Van's musical development because Berns had an intimate understanding of the music industry, and he was also an astute songwriter and producer. On a business trip to London, Berns confided to a promoter: "I've come over for Van Morrison, I'm going to bring him back to America to record and I guarantee he'll be on the charts within a month." This was the beginning of Van Morrison's solo career, and a personal odyssey which resulted in Van moving permanently to the United States.

After completing the 1966 American tour with Them, Van considered living in Northern California, but for economic reasons he soon abandoned the idea. Van should not have worried about money, because the rise of FM radio, the popularity of the Monterey Pop Festival, and the increase in signing new acts by the major record companies in 1967 was an indication that rock and roll music was no longer a suspect commodity in the record-ing industry. After RCA signed Elvis Presley in November, 1955, they did not sign another major rock act until the Jefferson Airplane in the mid-1960s. As a result 1967 was a banner year for new rock acts. The British invasion was three years old, and rock music had proven to be a highly successful part of the major record labels' profits. Warner Brothers was already talking with Van Morrison in 1967, but there were some personal ties between Van and Bert Berns. There was also a feeling in Van's mind that Berns was one of the few recording executives who understood his musical direction.

It was Berns' stature within the recording industry that convinced Van

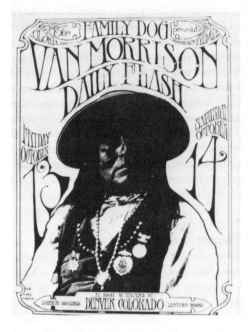

A poster advertising Van's appearance at The Family Dog in Denver, 1967.

to come to New York for a recording session. The 38 year old Berns had worked as a record salesman in the 1950s, but quickly became a session piano player, songwriter, and producer. In 1962 Berns brought the Isley Brothers "Twist and Shout" to a number of companies and eventually Florence Greenberg's Wand label released it. This established Berns as an important songwriter and soon Don Covay, Marv Johnson, Garnet Mimms, The Rocky Fellers and Conway Twitty recorded his songs. There was little doubt that Berns was not only a gifted writer, but also an astute judge of potential hit records. As a result of his varied skills, Berns founded the Web IV publishing company, and artists such as Barbara Lewis, Ben E. King, The Drifters, and Solomon Burke recorded Berns' tunes. In collaboration with Wes Farrell, Berns wrote the Vibrations' hit record, "My Girl Sloopy." In England Eric Clapton and the Yardbirds played this song nightly in London pubs. Van Morrison and Them also performed this tune. These credentials were important ones, and Van Morrison believed that Berns not only understood his music but that he would provide freedom in the recording studio.

When Bang Records was formed, Berns was able to consummate a promotion and distribution deal with Atlantic Records. As a result of these business arrangements, the label name BANG was the initials of the following Atlantic executives and Berns. The B was from Berns' name. The A was from Ahmet Ertegun, President of Atlantic Records. The N from

Nesuhi Ertegun who joined his younger brother Ahmet in 1955 at Atlantic Records. The G was from Gerald (Jerry) Wexler, a songwriter-producer at Atlantic. Although not a major label, Bang and its subsidiary, Shout, nevertheless had an excellent reputation among rising singers.

When Van Morrison arrived in New York in July, 1967, he believed that Bert Berns and Bang Records would provide a creative forum for his song-writing and performing talents. On a hot, muggy July 5th afternoon, Van took a taxi cab to mid-town Manhattan to record his initial tracks for Bang Records at the A & R and Century Sound Studios. The sessions which followed were intense, emotional, and often confused by Van's inability to bring the musicians to share his grasp of a song. Yet, despite all the tension, "Brown-Eyed Girl" emerged from this session as Van's first solo hit. But it was the five minute and eleven second version of "He Ain't Give You None" and the nine minute and forty-four second song "T.B. Sheets" which established the jazz-blues orientation of Van's music.

"Brown-Eyed Girl" was recorded in just two takes, and due to the late session, the backup singers, the Sweet Inspirations—Cissy Houston, Dee Dee Warwick and Myrna Smith—had returned to their hotel. As a result the background vocals were sung by Bert Berns, Jeff Berry, and Brooks Arthur. During this first session only three songs were completed, because after Van's extraordinary performance on "T.B. Sheets," the emotional drain prompted Berns to cancel the remainder of the session. Since "T.B. Sheets" was a song about a young girl Van had lived with and watched die of tuberculosis, there was a strong degree of sentiment during the last few hours of this session.

There was little doubt that the eight songs that Bang Records released on the Van Morrison album entitled *Blowin' Your Mind* were some of his finest early songwriting efforts. Since six of the album's eight songs were written by Van, he quickly became identified as a song poet. There was a lyrical skill in these songs which few American songwriters could match, and the depth of feeling in Van's work caught the attention of young musicians like Peter Wolf. In 1967 the Boston area was filled with innovative rock music, and the J. Geils Band formed around Wolf's vocals. It was Wolf who recognized Van's enormous talent and often sang "Brown-Eyed Girl." In 1978 Wolf was the emcee when Van broadcast a live show from the Bottom Line in New York City. In a quiet moment backstage Wolf told a rock journalist that no one blended more diverse influences in songwriting than Van Morrison.

In order to promote airplay for "Brown-Eyed Girl" and the *Blowin' Your Mind* album, Van began to tour with Charles Brown, a guitarist; Eric Oxendine, a bass player; and Bob Grenier, a drummer. Much to Van's horror, Bang Records was unable to escape the sleazy, second-rate clubs which had hindered the development of his music during the tours with Them. When someone in the crowd hollered "rock and roll" or "Gloria,"

Van often walked off the stage.

"Ro Ro Rosey" was Van's second 45 release for Bang Records, and it did not move up the *Billboard* charts. Reflecting on the *Blowin' Your Mind* album, Van commented, "I didn't think that album really had anything to do with where I was at." In his little notebook Van was already penning small phases and weaving subtle lyrics into the set of songs which would become *Astral Weeks*. Long before he signed his Warner Brothers contract, Van was creating the lyrical magic and the musically sophisticated songs which would bring instant stardom.

It was Van's second Bang album which caused most of the problems with the label. Bert Berns died of a heart attack on December 31, 1967 and Bang quickly released another album entitled *The Best of Van Morrison*. It was a hastily conceived and assembled project which included five songs from the *Blowin' Your Mind* album. This ended Van's association with Bang Records, for the executives who replaced Berns had no concept of the rock music world. Consequently, Van began to look around for a new record deal. The contradiction in Van's life was that he was a solo singer with a top ten hit and strong reviews as a song poet, but he was also an artist who believed that full creative freedom was difficult to obtain in the jungles of corporate rock and roll music.

Van Morrison was a successful solo recording artist in 1967 but the hit-making potential of "Brown-Eyed Girl" had failed to provide him the necessary freedom to develop his music. He was also agitated by the continual requests for personal appearances on shows like American Bandstand, but much to his credit Van was never personally critical of Dick Clark or other media figures who made their living in rock journalism. What Van despised was the constant demand that he do his songs the same way each time. Like many blues artists Van followed his personal feelings and this resulted in a number of different versions of his songs. "Every time I do a song," Van stated, "I do it differently. I just can't sing any song the same way twice." Although "Brown-Eyed Girl" reached number ten on the *Billboard* charts and remained there for sixteen weeks, Van was still unhappy with the compromises forced upon his music by Bang Records. Since Bert Berns had always concentrated upon Top 40 hit material, Van immediately found himself attempting to avoid this contrived sound. As a result there had been a constant clash of wills between Van and Berns. In retrospect, however, some of Van's more soulful early songs were recorded in the turmoil surrounding Bang Records.

The most significant Bang album is *T.B. Sheets*. Although not released until 1973, this collection of songs is Van's best early solo work. The liner notes on the album by Michael Ochs are extremely sophisticated and the fold-out cover provides an excellent picture of Van as well as the lyrics to his songs. In the studio Van usually cuts most tunes in two or three takes and the spontaneity of Van's recordings are evident in the eight songs on

T.B. Sheets. When he recorded for Bang Records, Van remarked to a reporter: "You don't understand me; but believe me, I know what I'm saying." This is a perfect summary of Van's difficulties in his early years in the record business. His sound was so unique and his songwriting talents so abstract and creative that the executives of many record companies found it difficult to find a suitable niche for Van's music. What the industry was not used to was a performer who was creative beyond the conventional bounds. It was obvious that a new record company was necessary for Van's musical development to continue.

It is difficult to analyze Van's solo career with Bang Records. Had it not been for the untimely death of Bert Berns, Van might have continued to turn out Top 40 hits. This seems unlikely though because there was a great deal of controversy over the direction of Van's music. Bert Berns was a genius when a two-and-a-half minute hit song was needed, but he proved less adept at producing the artistic rock and roll poems which formed the bulk of Van's music in 1967-1968. Yet the three Bang albums were an important reason for Van's development as a songwriter. While not given

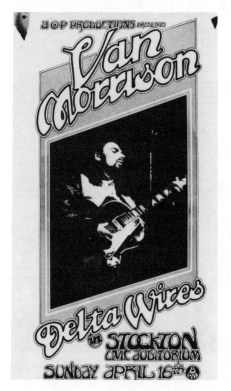

A poster advertising one of Van's performances in Stockton, California. From the early 1970s.

the creative freedom that he desired in the studio, Van was still able to craft a musical style which reflected the freedom of dress, manners and morals in American society during the late 1960s.

In late 1967 Van moved from New York to Cambridge, near Boston. The atmostphere surrounding Harvard University was a stimulating one and there were a number of small clubs where Van could perform. Van's growing unhappiness with Bang Records was an important reason for moving from New York, and in 1970 Van told a *Rolling Stone* reporter: "Bang Records was a mistake for me, it was the wrong label. That just wasn't my market."

There were some high points, however, in Van's brief recording career with Bang Records. On July 28, 1967 London Records in the United Kingdom issued "Brown-Eyed Girl" and there was a great deal of press coverage given to Van's solo career. This made Van feel vindicated because Them had received a lot of hostile publicity from the British press. In many respects the positive publicity generated for Van's early Bang Records in London helped to establish his European popularity.

Despite Van's misgivings the Bang Records experience was an integral part of his burgeoning career. There were a number of important musicians like Peter Wolf of the J. Geils Band who influenced the direction of Van's music. There were also many opportunities to share the stage with

Jeff Barry, Bert Berns, Van, Janet Planet and Dr. Sussel during the Bang Records promotional cruise down the Hudson River in 1967. *Photo courtesy Peter Kanze.*

newly emerging artists. One night in an obscure Cambridge club Van and Peter Wolf shared the stage and sang "Gloria" and "Brown-Eyed Girl" to an eager audience of about fifty people. There were also parties during the Bang Record period which offered Van a chance to integrate his musical ideas with producers, arrangers, songwriters and the press. Bert Berns hired a boat to cruise down the Hudson River in 1967 and this extraordinary press conference resulted in airplay and a great deal of media attention. Yet it was not the type of event which appealed to Van. As a result he confided to a friend, "I would have been better off on a blues label." There were a number of major record companies interested in Van and during December, 1967 several recording executives approached him.

Van Morrison: Warner Brothers and Astral Weeks, 1968

In 1968 Van Morrison signed a recording contract with Warner Brothers. There was very little publicity about Van's shift to a major label and there were no interviews. Warner Brothers shrewdly waited for Van's first record before they began to promote his music. The reasons that Van signed with Warner Brothers are not easily explained but his choice of labels was excellent. In the 1960s Warner Brothers' marketing strategy concentrated upon the college market and young working adults. Warner's production techniques were outstanding and the company prided itself on hiring executives who understood the rock and roll market.

When Warner Brothers bought Reprise Records from Frank Sinatra in 1963 they were able to turn an extraordinary profit. This established the Warner Brothers-Reprise label but it was a middle-of-the-road, pop company featuring artists like Dinah Shore, Sammy Davis and Dean Martin. The lure of the rock music market, however, soon prompted Warner Brothers to hire Joe Smith, a Boston disc jockey, as national promotion director, and he immediately signed the San Francisco-based Grateful Dead to a recording contract. Smith had scouted The Grateful Dead at a number of concerts in San Francisco's Avalon Ballroom. He realized that there was real potential in the rock market. Warner Brothers also had the rights to distribute The Kinks in America, and they began an aggressive program of issuing sampler albums with cuts by a number of artists. By advertising in small magazines and rock newspapers, Warner Brothers developed the reputation as the people's record label. Considering the trendy, counter-culture attitudes of the late 1960s, this was a shrewd business move. Using the pages of *Rolling Stone* magazine, Warner Brothers purchased full page ads suggesting that they were virtually giving their product away for a dollar or two. The sampler albums were very popular and they allowed record buyers to hear 11 to 22 artists on a single or double album.

When Warner Brothers signed Van Morrison it was due to Joe Smith, who eventually became president of Elektra Records. It was Smith who convinced skeptical corporate executives that Van had a unique style tailored for the musical tastes of the late 1960s. One of Smith's strongest arguments was that FM radio stations like San Francisco's KSAN were creating a demand for long-playing albums. The day of heavy 45 record sales was not over, but the increasingly sophisticated rock music purchaser demanded quality albums. The concept or rock opera album was developing and Van Morrison was to become one of the earliest artists to record a classic rock opera. Had it not been for Joe Smith's encouragement and support, Van's first project with Warner Brothers, *Astral Weeks*, might not have been completed.

It would have been difficult, if not impossible, to promote the *Astral Weeks* album had it not been for the rise of FM radio stations. In the mid-1960s FM radio began revolutionizing traditional rock and roll radio by challenging the staid playlists of AM Top 40 music. There was little variety in Top 40 programming and the music of Frank Zappa's Mothers of Invention, Captain Beefheart, Tim Buckley or Tracy Nelson's Mother Earth was not available to most listeners. Yet albums by these artists sold very well in the late 1960s and they played to well-attended concerts in all parts of the United States. Columbia Records recognized the importance of FM radio and began publishing an underground news sheet entitled *Keep Your Ear to the Ground*. It was sent to FM radio stations and head shops to promote records released by Columbia.

Bob Dylan, a Columbia artist, was the first FM radio superstar, and his music quickly crossed over to traditional AM stations. But Columbia was not the only company to realize that FM radio was a new forum for the rock music market. Warner Brothers hired 25 field representatives who began to distribute promotional items to important FM radio stations. The college market blended with the emerging counterculture and straight business types to make the recording industry a booming enterprise in the late 1960s. *Astral Weeks* became a favorite of most college radio stations and Warner Brothers advertised heavily in street weeklies and college newspapers to promote Van Morrison's music.

The most significant disc jockey in Van's career was San Francisco's Tom Donahue. In many respects Donahue's career is a microcosmic study of the origins and development of FM radio. In 1960 admist the well-publicized payola scandals, Donahue left WIBG to work at KYA in San Francisco. Although he was extremely successful as a disc jockey, Donahue also became financially independent due to the success of his recording company, Autumn Records. A man of tremendous intelligence and unflagging energy, Donahue recognized that the San Francisco area was a mecca for strug-

gling young musicians. He soon signed the Beau Brummels, Bobby Free-
man, the Great Society featuring Grace Slick and the Mojo Men. Sylvester
Stewart, a disc jockey at KDIA who later went on to stardom with Sly and
the Family Stone, was Donahue's chief producer. Autumn Records released 24 45 records, and 18 of them made the national *Billboard* charts.
But Donahue was not the traditional recording company executive. Often
he would arrive at a concert in a van and his 300 pound frame would
bounce out of the truck. On the side of the van was a sign reading "We Have
Come For Your Daughters." With a beard and a gigantic belly, Donahue
looked like a character in a B movie but his instincts were strictly for business. When one of his business partners died of cancer in 1966, Donahue retired for more than a year. He was able to do this because in addition to
promoting San Francisco's first Beatles' concert in Candlestick Park in
1964, his Autumn Records venture was successful. When Donahue returned to radio, however, he revolutionized the industry. It all began one
night when a friend of Donahue's came by and began talking about stereo
FM radio. Donahue remembers telling him, "I don't even have an FM
radio." After listening to a number of FM stations, Donahue called KMPX.
When a telephone operator came on the line and informed him that the
station's phone was disconnected, he knew that he could convince the
owner to hire him as disc jockey.

On April 7, 1967 Donahue began an eight to midnight shift on KMPX. He
soon became so successful that *Rolling Stone* magazine described AM radio
as "a rotting corpse stinking up the airwaves." Donahue wisely invested
his own money in KMPX and within a year a sister station, KPPC, was
opened in Pasadena. Thus began the FM progressive rock revolution and
Van Morrison was only one of many artists who benefitted from this new
format. It was not uncommon to tune in KMPX and hear an entire album.
There was no strict playlist and the DJ's were free to play and do whatever
they desired. FM became a highly profitable business and soon attracted
major radio conglomerates. One of the main reasons for the growth of FM
radio was the superiority of its sound over that of AM. This advantage was
subsequently increased by the introduction of multiplexing, a technical in-
novation which allowed the FM stations to transmit stereo musical broad-
casts. Soon 668 FM stations were broadcasting in stereo. This was the type
of radio sound which made it possible to enjoy every subtle nuance in Van
Morrison's *Astral Weeks* album.

Eventually Tom Donahue went to another San Francisco radio station,
KSAN, and built it into the major progressive rock station in the country. It
was possible to tune in KSAN and hear local Bay Area musicians playing
live concerts. Since there was no identifiable playlist, the music of Country
Joe and the Fish, the Charlatans, the Quicksilver Messenger Service, the
Moby Grape, Big Brother and the Holding Company, and Lamb offered
Bay Area listeners a wide variety of songs not available on AM.

Van in a publicity shot from the early 1970s.

Although FM radio was to prove important to Van's success as a solo artist, there was still a great deal of uncertainty about his future during the recording and promotion of *Astral Weeks*. "We faced an artist who had not been treated very well," remembered Joe Smith of Warner Brothers. Van was suspicious of production and technical people at Warner Brothers. Smith fought for Van's freedom in the studio and urged Warner Brothers to continue to provide the necessities of life for Van until his records became commercial successes. In the first three years with Warner Brothers, Van only recorded two albums. Recently one rock critic suggested that *Astral Weeks* was recorded in 48 hours. This may be accurate because Van is noted for completing a song in two or three takes. However, it ignores the months and often years that Van scribbles in his notebook and quietly experiments with songs. In later years Van revealed that *Astral Weeks* was written in Ireland and England. Long before he signed with Warner Brothers Van had written and structured the basic concept behind the album. He often remarked that his notebook was something that the other members of Them could not understand. But FM radio listeners and the older disc jockeys who were refugees from Top 40 playlists came to love the lyrical and poetic skills of Van Morrison.

There was also a business revolution in the recording industry. No longer were most artists forced to negotiate for each 45 record release or album contract. Warner Brothers began to sign a large number of artists to long-term contracts. RCA had only one or two significant rock acts. In 1956 RCA's president was a classical music buff and he believed that Elvis Presley was the only rock singer necessary to the label's success. It was not until 1965 that RCA signed its second rock group, the Jefferson Airplane. But Warner Brothers realized that the rock and roll market was extremely lucrative. As a result they signed artists like Van Morrison to long-term contracts. Since many songwriters make a large portion of their income from publishing rights, it was essential to guarantee ASCAP and BMI royalties. Many composers referred to these payments as "old age money." It was Joe Smith who convinced Warner Brothers to guarantee Van Morrison the type of contract which made the label an artist-oriented one. That is, a contract which provided for comfortable living as well as money for creative experimentation in the recording studio.

In a reflective interview, Joe Smith recalled his early meetings with Van Morrison in a small Boston club in 1967. Smith remembered that Van had immigration problems and that he believed Bang Records was merchandising his records in the wrong market. When *Astral Weeks* was completed, Smith realized that it would not be an immediate best seller. However, he convinced skeptical Warner Brothers management that the album's sales would be steady for a number of years. The first year *Astral Weeks* sold only 15,000 copies but 10,000 of these were merchandised in Los Angeles and San Francisco. It was five years before *Astral Weeks* sold more than a

100,000 copies but the album continues to sell well into the 1980s.

Warner Brothers did not release *Astral Weeks* until November, 1968 and there was only a minimal amount of publicity surrounding the album. But great care was taken in preparation for the album's production. The session musicians were carefully selected for their diversity and innovative musical talents. The drummer, Connie Kay, had worked with the Modern Jazz Quartet. The bass player, Richard Davis, was an excellent studio jazz musician. The guitarist, Jay Berliner, was a jazz musician and John Payne was a singer-songwriter who had played with Van in the Boston area. To assist in production Warner Brothers assigned Lewis Merenstein to oversee *Astral Weeks*. There was a great deal of turmoil within the studio for a period of time and Van eventually shut himself into a production studio with only his guitar and notebook. John Cale, who was recording in an adjoining studio, remarked that Van was a loner who worked diligently on *Astral Weeks*. It may have been recorded in 48 hours as was suggested, but Van worked with a great deal of discipline for years on the project. In fact, in 1972 Van told a *Rolling Stone* reporter that this album "was different from the things I'd recorded previously but it didn't really represent a period of change in my life."

For a number of years Van had worked on a rock opera album concept. As a result of this interest Van entitled side A "In The Beginning" and side B "Afterwards." Long before The Who or The Moody Blues were popularizing the rock opera, Van created and recorded the intricate selection of sounds and musical ideas behind the rock opera story line. In 1968 no one was successfully carrying a single theme through an album. That changed with the release of *Astral Weeks*.

Although a hit single did not emerge from the album, Van was "pretty happy with the album." Despite some tension during the recording session Van remarked: "One thing I gotta admit, Warner Brothers has given me complete artistic control." This comment was made some time after *Astral Weeks* but it demonstrates the concern which Warner Brothers showed for a new and basically unknown solo artist.

The tour to promote the album was a simple one. The presence of only two backup musicians resulted in bookings in small clubs. This is what Van preferred and he gave his best performances at bars with egg cartons on the ceilings to muffle the acoustics. Van remarked after playing Pauley Pavilion, the home of UCLA's basketball team, that he realized the big auditorium was not the place for his music. The artistic success of Van's *Astral Weeks* tour was noted in underground newspapers like the *Berkeley Barb*, the *Los Angeles Free Press* and the *Village Voice*. These reviews persuaded Warner Brothers to continue to provide for Van's necessities and to encourage further development of his music.

During the tour Van met The Band in Los Angeles and he eventually moved to their hometown of Woodstock, New York. In 1971 The Band's

Cahoots album featured a song, "4% Pantomime," written by Van and The Band's Robbie Robertson. It was the first song that Van had composed with another artist. In addition to jamming with The Band, Van also played with Bob Dylan and other musicians around Woodstock. As a result of *Astral Weeks* Van was able to lease a small farmhouse in the area in 1969. The Woodstock environment was a very creative one and he did not leave it until 1972 when he moved to Mill Valley in Marin County north of San Francisco. In 1968-1969 Van was establishing his career as a major creative solo artist. It had been almost a decade since his musical odyssey began with The Monarchs and the success of *Astral Weeks* was a significant turning point in his development as a songwriter.

Despite the artistic success of his first Warner Brothers album, Van was determined to gain stronger controls in the studio. One of the reasons for this was that Warner Brothers had placed the last song on *Astral Weeks* without Van's approval. This led to the exclusion of two key songs from the album. As a result, "Slim Slow Slider" was the last tune and Van believed it was the wrong type of song to end the album. Greil Marcus in the March 1, 1969 issue of *Rolling Stone* called Astral Weeks "profoundly intellectual" but when the critics heaped too much praise on Van, he quietly set them in their places. John Tobler, an English journalist for *Zig Zag* magazine informed Van that he found *Astral Weeks* "messianic." Van replied, "I think it's all in your head." Even though Van had achieved enormous commercial popularity he was able to maintain a balanced perspective on the rock music world.

There are a number of indications that Van's earlier songs helped to form the nucleus of *Astral Weeks*. The lyrics to "Little Girl," written in 1965 during his years with Them, are similar to lines in "Cyprus Avenue." The setting and themes in "Madame George" are constant reminders of Van's Belfast days. When Van sang the blues with Them and performed traditional rock and roll music, his songwriting skills were much like those exhibited in the *Astral Weeks* album. Consequently his first Warner Brothers album was a continuation of themes and ideas which had ripened for years in Van's mind. Yet there was a change coming over Van's music and he was about to enter the most commercially successful phase of his musical career.

Van Morrison: From Moondance to Tupelo Honey, 1969-1971

In 1969 Van began to tour with a newly formed six piece band. As a result of the traditional rock and roll training of these new musicians, Van's music had a honky tonk, good-time quality to it but Van continued to experiment with new musical ideas. He did not restrict himself to a single band or one musical style. Perhaps the best example of Van's innovative approach to his music occurred when he played the Gaslight Club and the Catacombs in Boston with Bob Kilbania on upright bass and John Payne on flute. After opening at the Catacombs with "Cypress Avenue" Van performed an elaborate set which combined poetic mysticism with rock and roll music. Yet, there was a diversity and intellectual quality to Van's music which was not apparent in most other artists' work. Warner Brothers quickly recognized this talent and sent Van out on a brief tour of rock clubs and colleges. Almost immediately the loose, long song poems captivated a new generation of students. But Van also had a rock and roll direction as evidenced by the *Moondance* album.

When *Moondance* was recorded in 1969 there were a number of important influences on Van's music. Not only did he substantially depart from the mystical qualities of the *Astral Weeks* album, Van also brought a number of new musicians into his band. Jack Schroer's alto and soprano saxophones, Jef Labes' piano and organ, John Platania's lead and rhythm guitar work, and Colin Tillton's flute added a new dimension to Van's music. The addition of veteran singer Judy Clay as well as Emily Houston and Jackie Verdell on backup vocals added a hard-driving rhythm and blues tone to the *Moondance* album. The commercial qualities of Van's albums from 1969 to 1971 were extremely important in establishing him as a well-known recording artist. Warner Brothers released a number of 45 records and in 1970-1971 five of Van's 45 record releases made the *Billboard* charts and the three albums released from 1969-1971 all fared well on the charts. There was also an increased demand for live appearances.

In 1970 the demand for Van's music reached a fever point. Not only did he play to standing room only crowds at Bill Graham's Fillmore East, but the concert was broadcast live over the National Educational Television Network. This show featured The Byrds, Sha Na Na, and the Elvin Bishop group. When Van concluded the Fillmore East show with a hard-driving version of "Cypress Avenue" many of the fans who listened intently to the *Astral Weeks* album were surprised by the uptempo, rock and roll version of the song. Although Van was visibly nervous during the television special, he delivered a moving performance. At the end of his set Van cut the microphone off and threw it to the floor. He then walked off the stage. It was symbolic of Van's feelings as he preferred the small clubs and the lack of adulation. This was a means of cutting himself off from the audience and it indicated Van's strong desire to retain his personal and artistic freedom.

There was little doubt that *Moondance* indicated a highly commercial direction for Van's music. At Boston's Symphony Hall in 1970 Van blended blues songs with his newly released material and was in charge of an ecstatic crowd. This was generally the case in 1970 and 1971 as Van was able to direct his music to highly pleased audiences. When the *Moondance* album reached number 29 on the *Billboard* charts and a single, "Come Running," hit number 39 on the 45 charts there was little doubt about Van's hit-making potential. There was an incredible staying power to Van's music that was demonstrated when "Moondance" turned up again for a short time in 1977 in the number 92 position on the *Billboard* 45 charts.

There is also a simplistic maturity to *Moondance*. The opening song, "And It Stoned Me," is typical of the influence of nature. Van weaves a story of freedom standing in the rain and he communicates a feeling of personal euphoria produced by the countryside. The English rock magazine *Melody Maker* called *Moondance* "the solidest rock achievement thus far in 1970." Despite heavy touring commitments, Van continued fervently to write new songs.

Van during the aftermath of *Astral Weeks*.

It was in Woodstock that Van was able to hide from the glare of the rock and roll spotlight and write the music to the album, *His Band and the Street Choir*. In this album the Caledonia Soul Orchestra became Van's new backup band. In reality, this group was partly familiar and partly new musicians combined into a more flexible and wide-ranging group. It was not uncommon for Van to blend jazz, blues, folk and traditional rock and roll music into a set. This album rose to number 32 on the *Billboard* charts in 1971 and Van's best selling 45, "Domino," reached number nine on the charts. "Blue Money" was number 23 and "Call Me Up In Dreamland" briefly entered the *Billboard* ratings at number 95. These three singles guaranteed Van's commercial future with Warner Brothers. His artistic achievements were already recognized throughout the music industry.

The success of *His Band and the Street Choir* was due to a unique combination of themes involving music, life, happiness, sorrow and reflections on a changing world. There is a hint of turmoil in "Domino" when Van complains of the constant swirl of show business and the need for a rest. In other tunes such as "I've Been Working," Van reflects on the work and a woman's place in his life. In "Blue Money" Van tells a simple story of a young girl doing some quick pornographic modeling for a small bit of spending money. It is a small moment in someone's life but a slice of American life, a poet's musing look at an intriguing incident.

The popularity of FM radio continued to affect Van's success. In San Francisco, pioneer disc jockey Tom Donahue had become a nationally recognized authority on "underground radio" and played a great deal of Van's music. "He's got the lyrics that remind you of generations of hard times and misery and that kind of black Irish soul," Donahue remarked. Once "Domino" began to climb the *Billboard* charts, Van faced the pressures of stardom. It was difficult to cope with the constant attention, the demand for incessant media interviews, and the continual pressure by Warner Brothers to go out on tour. In addition, the lease on Van's house in Woodstock ran out and this made it easier to consider moving to San Francisco.

It was a natural move for Van Morrison. His wife, Janet Planet, graduated from high school in San Rafael, north of San Francisco and Van had enjoyed the concerts he had given at the Fillmore West. "I'd always wanted to move to California," Van remembered but he had also enjoyed the Woodstock environment. Robbie Robertson of The Band was a close friend and there were many musicians to jam with during free moments. In Marin County there were also many professional musicians who had gravitated to California in the aftermath of the Summer of Love in 1967 in San Francisco's Haight-Ashbury district. The myths about California's freedoms were far greater than rumored and often the dream turned to nightmare as evidenced by Janis Joplin's and Mike Bloomfield's tragic deaths. Yet in general, Marin County was a haven for experimental musicians of all persuasions. Mark Naftalin, the keyboardist in the Paul Butterfield Blues Band, settled in Marin. Nick Gravenites came west in 1967 from Chicago. Janis Joplin frequently dropped into small clubs like The Sweetwater to listen to local bands. Janis' first group, Big Brother and the Holding Company, were Marin residents. The Quicksilver Messenger Service, Clover, the Moby Grape, the Steve Miller Band and many others at one time or another lived in and around Mill Valley in Marin County.

There was much the same feeling in the small community of Mill Valley as Van had experienced living in Woodstock. Not only was there a rustic, country feeling to life, but there was a sense of art and experimental music. The move to a small house in Mill Valley was a positive one. The home had a swimming pool and Van was able to install a 16 track recording studio in the garage. One of the bedrooms was converted into a sauna and the ethos of a health food oriented society began to creep into Van's consciousness. There were also some exciting new places to perform in in and around San Francisco.

As the interest in Van's music grew it was only logical that unauthorized bootleg albums would begin to appear in San Francisco record stores. In October, 1971 a bootleg LP entitled *Van the Man* appeared in Leopold's record store in Berkeley. A unique record store, Leopold's was originally a student-owned store near the University of California campus. Unlike traditional corporate record stores, Leopold's staff were shrewd judges of commercially successful music. It became the first San Francisco area store to feature Van Morrison recordings extensively. The *Van the Man* bootleg had a white cover with a xeroxed insert and the album production itself was terrible. However, the sound quality was excellent because it was recorded at the Fillmore West in 1970 and at Pacific High Studios in October of 1971. The following month, November, 1971, Van Morrison broadcast a show on FM station KSAN from the Pacific High studios and a second bootleg album called *The Belfast Cowboy* appeared in local stores. There were some surprising songs on the bootleg albums. "Hound Dog," the tune made famous by Elvis Presley, provided an excellent example of Van's rock and roll roots. Bob Dylan's "Just Like A Woman" was an immediate hit from the *Van the Man* album. Local San Francisco FM radio stations began to play cuts from the bootlegs and Van Morrison's California popularity showed recognition of his artistic and musical skill.

There were also some new found pressures in the San Francisco rock music world. In November, 1971 while performing on Bill Graham's Winterland stage, Van became frightened when the sound system suddenly went dead. He had a delayed reaction to the overcrowded and often vocally expressive Winterland audience. Despite Bill Graham's excellent professional handling of a heavily attended concert, Van began to have some doubts about the rock music scene. Not only did the crowd continually holler for "Gloria" and "Here Comes The Night" but they seemed to drain the

Van in concert in the early 1970s. *Photo courtesy Chris Bradford*

creative forces of a performer with constant demands for new songs. Once
the sound system gave way, Van simply walked off the stage. When the
sound was restored he refused to return. Mark Naftalin, the piano player,
urged Van to return to the stage. Finally Mark and Taj Mahal coaxed Van
back out and he finished the show with "Blue Money" and "Domino." The
ecstatic crowd rushed the stage and nubile little nymphets danced on the
corners of the stage as Van moved to the back of the spacious auditorium.
This incident was the beginning of a withdrawn stage personality which
has characterized Van Morrison for more than a decade. The pressures of
the rock music business were getting to Van and in a moment of rare
candor he told a *Los Angeles Times* reporter that he was tired of touring and
mindlessly performing his hit records.

One of the ways in which Van combatted the frustrations of the rock
music world was to emphasize the lyrics in "Domino." In words which
were hints at his future lifestyle, Van wrote "I'll go underground, Get some
heavy rest, Never have to worry about what is worst and what is best."
Although he threatened to retire and convinced a few journalists that he
had left the music business, Van continued to tour and record. But the incident at Winterland was an indication of some changes in Van's professional and personal life.

Perhaps the most significant change in Van's professional life was the new found joy of playing small clubs. Although Van began his career in small bars playing cover tunes, he had drifted away from the intimate little clubs. This changed in October of 1971 when he performed a live show for 200 people at Pacific High Recorders which was broadcast over KSAN. It was a mellow, often intimate experience which allowed Van to experiment with songs like "Que Sera Sera" as well as to feel the response of a quiet and appreciative crowd. Unlike the Fillmore Auditorium no one hollered "rock and roll, man." It was the intellectual side to Van's performing nature which prompted him to search out the small clubs.

In December, 1971 Van paid his way into the Lion's Share in San Anselmo, California to see Ramblin' Jack Elliott. After some coaxing, Ramblin' Jack brought Van on stage for a couple of songs. Once he stood in front of the fifty people at the Lion's Share Van was hooked on the intimacy and the freedom of a small club. Eventually Van played the Lion's Share as a solo artist accompanied only by his acoustic guitar. A small Marin County radio station announced in 1971 that Van would play the Lion's Share and three dollar tickets were available at the club. Within two hours the show was sold out. In the age of corporate rock it is uncommon for an artist to play to a crowd of fans for a few dollars. But this type of performance is what keeps Van Morrison's music creative and artistic.

As Van performed on the stage of the Lion's Share, blues guitarist John Lee Hooker walked in and joined Van on stage for a couple of songs. As a result Van eventually played on two of John Lee Hooker's albums, *Never Get Out of These Blues Alive* and *Born in Mississippi and Raised in Tennessee*. In the 1980s Van continues to play small halls like the San Francisco Great ˙ American Music Hall. This beautiful structure seats only 480 people but the acoustics and the art deco interior make it a perfect place to perform.

As a result of his musical breadth and diversity and his penchant for perfection, Van Morrison has a reputation for not being easy to work with. Ben Fong-Torres wrote in *Rolling Stone* that "Morrison is the consummate music maker, a tyrant when it comes to putting his bands together, an introspective, unpredictable little ball of fire onstage." While there is an element of truth in this comment, it ignores the diversity and changeable nature of Van's music. Mark Jordan, who played piano with Van and later joined Dave Mason's band remarked: "Van's ability as a musician, arranger and producer is one of the scariest things I've seen. He hates to do retakes."

In the 1970s Tony Dey was a drummer who toured with Van but never recorded on any of his albums. A quiet, cultured Englishman, Dey began his career with Linda Ronstadt's Stone Ponies and later played with Lee Michaels. He remembers that Van usually cut a song in three or four takes and that many rehearsals were at three or four o'clock in the morning in Sausalito. At these sessions Van might begin playing a tune like The Drifters' "Under The Boardwalk." Sometimes he would start a set with

Little Willie John's "Fever." "There was little doubt that Van was heavily influenced by rock music pioneers," Dey remembered. Yet Dey also remembers playing "T.B. Sheets" for half an hour and he believes that this is the essence of Van's art. The ability to change his musical direction is the reason Van has remained so creative.

When Van and Janet Planet settled into a modest house on a hill in Mill Valley, life appeared to be an idyllic experience. Despite the constant pressures of touring and songwriting, Van was able to find friends, small clubs to perform in and an atmosphere conducive to his music. Van's two children, Peter and Shana, soon settled into a lifestyle where they chased a fifty pound cat affectionately named Sherwood around the Marin countryside. On Sunday afternoons Van could wander around the rustic hills or hear local groups like Barbara Mauritz' Lamb, Clover, or Asleep At The Wheel. During his early years in Marin County Van loved to watch Tom Salisbury who was the keyboardist for Lamb. Although Lamb recorded for Warner Brothers they never made it in the music business and Van reflected on the talent of his neighbors as he continued to develop his songwriting skills. The significance of Marin County is that it provided an eclectic influence on Van's music.

Jon Landau perfectly summarized Van when he wrote in *Rolling Stone*: "When Van Morrison starts burning, it is without the mannerisms and posturings we have come to associate with stars...He simply stands in front of his band, guitar in hand, and sings." But there were other concerns for Van. He remembered his long days on the road with Them and he did not have particularly fond memories of his recording career with Bang Records. Although he believed that Bern Berns was a musical genius, Van realized that proper business organization was necessary to protect and promote his growing cache of songs. Van began to look into forming his own production company.

In 1971 Van formed Caledonia Productions to merchandise and promote his songs properly. Initially, Caledonia Productions was set up to develop a network of musical talent. However, much of the company's energy went into producing Van's next four albums. The success of *Tupelo Honey, St. Dominic's Preview, Hard Nose The Highway*, and *It's Too Late To Stop Now* was a direct result of Van's driving artistic imput. In addition to promoting Van's music, Caledonia Productions also issued a professionally produced pamphlet entitled *Van Morrison: Reliable Sources*. This seventy-plus page book provides some interesting insights into Van's career. Not only does it include concert and record reviews which Van believed were the most accurate ones describing his career, but this excellent little book contains a number of pages from Van's journal. As one reads these entries it is possible to gain a window into Van's surrealistic thoughts. The stream of consciousness entries indicate that Van still keeps in touch with old friends in London and Belfast. There are also some indications that his musical inspira-

Van singing at the Circle Star Theater
in San Carlos, California, 1973. *Photo
courtesy Chris Bradford*

tion comes from Europe and not the United States.

When Caledonia Productions became involved in the *Tupelo Honey* album there were some tensions within Warner Brothers. Despite the success of this album, Van never believed that Warner Brothers promoted it adequately. In October, 1971 Warner released *Tupelo Honey*, Van's third album for the label in less than two years. This album reached number 27 on the *Billboard* charts and "Wild Night," and "Tupelo Honey" rose to numbers 28 and 47, respectively, on the 45 charts. "Wild Night" was a song written after a night out in New York and it showed Van's ability to take a common incident and write a poignant song based on his experience.

The musical explosion in Marin County also added a great deal to Van's music. In particular, Ronnie Montrose's excellent guitar work made *Tupelo Honey* a rock classic. Montrose, who had played with the Edgar Winter Group, was now a member of his own group entitled Gamma. Luis Gasca of El Chicano and John McFee of Clover were also additions to the *Tupelo Honey* musicians. Ted Templeman, who had played with Harper's Bizarre and would later go on to produce Van Halen, was responsible for the tightest production that Van experienced in the early 1970s. In an interview in *BAM* magazine, a Berkeley-based, northern California music magazine, Templeman recalled that Van was an iconoclast. "He's like... J.D. Salinger, he doesn't do things the way other writers do," Templeman remarked. "I had trouble with Van because he'd change his mind all the time." Yet Templeman credits Van with teaching him the value of spontaneous performance. When Templeman concluded his interview he informed the *BAM* reporter, "I'd never work with Van Morrison again as long as I live, even if he offered me $3 million in cash. I aged ten years producing three of his albums." Templeman credited Van's enormous talent but he found he was unable to work with him in the studio. Templeman attempted to withdraw these remarks in a subsequent issue of *BAM* and there were rumors that Templeman and Jerry Wexler were going to co-produce Van's next album. What this story suggests is that the intense pressure of making records creates tensions that the artist and producer often find impossible to bear. Perhaps Templeman was unable to understand the intensely personal nature of Van's music. He once remarked that Van called him up at three o'clock in the morning to let him know that one of his mixes was better than the one released on the "Tupelo Honey" 45. It was a clash between Templeman's structured life and Van's extraordinarily personal manner of making music.

In sum, Van's career from 1969 to 1971 was extremely productive. Not only did he produce three excellent albums but six songs from those LPs made the *Billboard* charts. This was Van's rock and roll period, and his music reflected the good-time atmosphere of his life both in Marin County and Woodstock.

Van Morrison: Experimentation and the Drift From Rock Music, 1972-1976

During the period from 1972 to 1976 Van intensified his musical experimentation and he also experienced some drastic changes in his lifestyle. Not only did Van go through an emotionally taxing divorce but his music demonstrated stronger jazz-blues tones. In many respects this was not a change, but simply a return to a previous style. Although Van's music had never been strictly rock and roll directed, both the *Moondance* and *Tupelo Honey* albums established Van strongly on the *Billboard* rock charts.

In June, 1972 Warner Brothers released the *St. Dominic's Preview* album. *Rolling Stone* called the album "the best produced, most ambitious Van Morrison yet released." In addition to the Caledonia Soul Orchestra, Van used Mark Naftalin on keyboards, Ron Elliot, a guitarist from The Beau Brummels and Jules Broussard, a jazz saxophonist who appeared on a number of Boz Scaggs' albums. This blend of blues piano, rock guitar and jazz saxophone resulted in a musical direction quite different from Van's past work.

An important reason for the unique sound of *St. Dominic's Preview* was due to the fact that it was recorded in San Francisco. Not only were Marin County musicians used but there was a new sense of freedom for Van in the studio.

There was also a unique experiment on side one of the album. The song "Listen To The Lion" opens with a slowly paced guitar which intensifies as Van sings about the lion inside each person. The ebb and flow of "Listen To The Lion" is an eleven minute musical exercise in which Van's growling vocals reach a crescendo peak and the listener is transported into a type of musical naturalism unfamiliar to the rock world.

As a result of these exciting musical directions, the *St. Dominic's Preview* album was Van's best selling career album. It rose to number 15 on the *Billboard* album listings and remained on the charts for 28 weeks. In addition, two singles, "Jackie Wilson Said" and "Redwood Tree" made the *Billboard* Hot 100. Many FM stations however, concentrated upon "Almost Independence Day," a ten minute, three second song which proclaimed Van's new sense of freedom. There were many changes in Van's life and this was reflected in his music. No longer was Van singing of love, relationships and good times. He seemed almost nostalgic in songs like "Gypsy." This tune commemorated the influence of Curtis Mayfield and the Impressions. But a tune like "Redwood Tree" allowed Van to recall his Irish youth, his love for nature and his yearning to find new meaning in the midst of a tempestuous time in his life.

In June, 1972 Van embarked on a tour to promote *St. Dominic's Preview*. When asked why he was going out on tour, Van replied to a reporter, "I want to play the music for the people to hear...that's it, the music and the people." In addition to these feelings Van needed to promote the album and to build his financial resources for a future hiatus from the music business. In a number of press conferences and interviews, Van was extremely critical of the music business and the pressures it generated on the performing artist. It was to be another two years before Van retired from recording and large concerts but he was already planning his sabbatical from the business.

There were some noticeable changes in Van's concerts. He had developed a strong stage shyness due to the pressures of the recording industry. "He was terrified at the sight of crowds one night," Mark Naftalin remarked, "but the next night he was oblivious to the pressures of a frenetic audience." Van recognized the problems of live performances and reflected on his stage jitters. "Sometimes it's really hard to get on," Van said, "I almost withdraw before I go on." It was Van's stage shyness, combined with the pressures of the industry which lead him to begin managing his own career. As his own personal manager, Van could select the small clubs and concert halls best suited to his performing style. The choice of concert facilities was often reflected in the reviews. On May 18, 1972 for example, Van performed an extraordinary set at Washington's fabled Constitution

44

Hall. Not only were there four standing ovations, Van repeatedly brought the crowd to its feet with his soaring vocals. Throughout the remainder of 1972 Van continued to tour and write songs. It was a busy and productive period in his professional life.

By 1973 there was an increasingly obvious mysticism creeping back into Van's music. It was a mystical vein similar to that of the poet W.B. Yeats. As a number of personal crises set in, Van recalled the "Caledonian Myths" of Scotland and often remarked that this land, which in ancient times had escaped Roman occupation for so long, was his mystical home. In 1973 Van's parents, George and Violet Morrison, moved to Marin County and his two year old daughter Shana was delighted to see her grandparents. During frequent family gatherings, Van often sat with Shana and watched "Sesame Street." As a result of watching a puppet called Kermit the Frog sing a song about "being green," Van recorded "Green." It was the first song he had recorded by another artist while on the Warner Brothers label.

In July, 1973 Warner Brothers released the *Hard Nose The Highway* album. In addition to the Caledonia Soul Orchestra, Van brought the Oakland Symphony Chamber Chorus in for background vocals. There was a jazz tone to this album and it included some unique string arrangements. There was also a tune, "Autumn Song," which was more than ten minutes long and indicated a pastoral direction to Van's music.

During both 1973 and 1974 Van toured Europe and America extensively. The result of these tours was an excellent live album entitled *It's Too Late*

Van performing at the Odyssey Room in Sunnyvale, California in 1973.
Photo courtesy Chris Bradford

A light moment in an interview with Ray Carr of England's *New Musical Express*.

To Stop Now. Warner Brothers released this double record set in February of 1974. It included concerts recorded on location during the summer of 1973 at Doug Weston's Troubadour Club in Los Angeles. There were also concert portions from the Santa Monica Civic Auditorium in California and from the Rainbow Theater in London. In addition to the Caledonia Soul Orchestra, Van hired Nathan Rubin, concert master of the Oakland Symphony Orchestra, on first violin. Ted Templeman provided excellent production and this album showcased Van's love of blues and early rock music by including songs by Sonny Boy Williamson, Sam Cooke, Ray Charles and Willie Dixon. The inclusion of musicians like Nathan Rubin as well as three violins, a viola, and cello was hardly typical of rock and roll music in the early 1970s and Van's eclectic selection of music was another sign of his independence.

In 1973 Van believed that the Caledonia Soul Orchestra was at its peak as a musical unit. "I was beginning to realize that there was nothing else to do within that particuar context," Van told Ray Carr of the *New Musical Express*. "What people didn't realize was that we had been doing practically the same show for five years and that by the time we came to Europe the only difference was the addition of the string section."

The tour which produced the live double album was the most successful of Van's career. The William Morris agency was beseeched with requests for Van to continue the tour. However, he had recently gone through a very draining divorce and his daughter, Shana, was on the tour. The settlement agreement was one which allowed Van visiting rights and he preferred to return to California to be near his daughter. It was not only his dislike for touring but his commitment to his children which took Van off the road after the live album was completed. There were very tempting financial offers but Van was intent upon continuing his musical growth and and maintaining a solid relationship with his children. He also was concerned that his music would become stagnant and predictable.

Despite Van's belief that his music was no longer as spontaneous as in the past, there is good evidence to indicate that he continued to effectively experiment in small clubs. On Sunday, April 22, 1973 for example, Van appeared with Jackie DeShannon at the Lion's Share in San Anselmo. This small club with a 150 seat capacity was treated to an extraordinary show as John Lee Hooker and Alice Stuart dropped in to add their blues and folk touches to Van's music. In August, 1973 Van performed two dynamic sets at the Santa Monica Civic Auditorium and then dropped by the Troubadour to hear Donald Byrd and Melissa Manchester. This was a time of exhaustion for Van and he soon contemplated new musical directions.

In 1974 it was obvious that the strain of touring, playing TV shows, writing and recording was taking its toll on Van. He was no longer as successful on the *Billboard* charts as he had been in the past. Moreover, there were rumors of tension between Van and Ted Templeman. Eventually they

Van at the Circle Star Theater, San Carlos, California in 1973. *Photo courtesy Chris Bradford*

parted company and the Caledonia Soul Orchestra was disbanded. The new touring group included Pete Wingfield on piano, Jerome Rinson on bass, and Dallas Taylor on drums. During this period Van played the Montreux Jazz Festival and briefly toured Ireland. A European 45 record release of the old Louis Jordan song, "Caledonia" did very well on the charts in Holland. There were also rumors that Van had recorded an album with the Crusaders but had decided not to release it. Al Kooper was also be lieved to have completed a rhythm and blues oriented album with Van. Bill Wyman, bass guitarist of The Rolling Stones, was also suspected of collaborating with Van on a project. These rumors were never verified but they were an indication of some serious changes in Van's music.

When *Veedon Fleece* was released in 1974 there was a mystical and detached quality to it. Not since *Astral Weeks* had Van written such abstract lyrics and he traveled to Ireland for inspiration. *Veedon Fleece* may have been a personal success for Van but it was obtuse and often difficult to interpret. As a result, it did not sell very well and Van did not tour extensively to support it. After a decade in midst of a volatile rock and roll world, Van was ready for a brief sabbatical. For some time he had been considering retirement and he announced to the press that it was time for a rest.

Although there was a two and a half year period between the release of *Veedon Fleece* and his next album, *A Period of Transition*, Van's retirement was in some ways a myth. He continued to play small clubs, write songs and work in his recording studio in Marin County. In 1975 and 1976 Tony Dey was Van's drummer. "He is a poet," Tony said, reflecting on Van's music. "A writer of words, but not a super musician. It is his words and his phrasing which make him unique," he concluded. During his tenure with Van Morrison Tony recalled that Van often played small clubs in Santa Barbara, Cotati and Santa Cruz. Many times Dey would be called to Marin County to do a recording session at two or three o'clock in the morning.

A reflective moment during the *It's Too Late to Stop Now* live album recordings. *Photo courtesy Don West*

"Van liked to do a song in two takes and this placed enormous responsibilities on the musicians," Dey stated. During his performances with Van, Dey provided a swing shuffle type of drum sound and this fit perfectly into Van's shows during 1975 and 1976. There were also long periods when Van traveled to Europe or returned to Belfast to be with friends. For the first time in his life Van Morrison was living as an average person. He enjoyed the time to travel, read, and consequently matured as an artist.

In 1976 Van was seen driving around Marin County in a rented Mercedes Benz with the personalized license plates "R and B" to signify rhythm and blues. Not only did Van continue to play new music, he became very close with a number of musicians from Jesse Colin Young's band. James Rothermel had a strong influence on Van's music which continued to grow in the mid-1970s. On the road Van had his road manager, Fast Freddie, set up a $5000 cassette unit and he continually listened to blues tunes or rhythm and blues on the Chess, King, or Federal labels. On a number of occasions in 1975 and 1976 Van simply wandered into a club where friends were playing and joined the band with his saxophone. It was a time of reflection, rest, and ultimately artistic regeneration.

On Thanksgiving night in 1976 The Band performed their final concert at Bill Graham's Winterland auditorium. The Last Waltz was the designation that Graham gave this event and he provided a star-studded lineup as well as a turkey dinner for the crowd. One of the guests at the Last Waltz was Van Morrison. As the concert unfolded Van casually walked through the crowd and was almost unnoticed by the reveling throng. When Van finally came on stage it was a magic moment. Not only did he fit perfectly into the nights's music but his version of "Caravan" turned an average show into a celebration. Greil Marcus in *Rolling Stone* magazine speculated that Van should have been one of the featured singers in The Band. "Why didn't he join The Band years ago?" Marcus mused. The appearance with The Band was an important turning point in Van's professional life. He was well received by the crowd and he suddenly demonstrated a renewed interest in live concerts.

During his year in England Van did attempt to get back into the recording studio. Prior to the Last Waltz he booked a studio in London. Rory Gallagher was one of the musicians who was hired to support Van's session. On a rainy evening Van entered the studio and looked at the set-up. "It looks fine," Van remarked. "Just a moment, I'll be right back." Van walked outside, hailed a cab and was taken to Heathrow Airport. He took the next plane for San Francisco. This ended Van's London exile and he returned to Marin County eager to renew his musical career. Although Van had lived sporadically in both Marin and London since 1974, he was ready to resume a full time California life.

Van's dynamic performance at The Last Waltz in San Francisco, November, 1976. *Photo courtesy Larry Hulst*

Bob Dylan, Robbie Robertson and Van at The Last Waltz. *Photo courtesy American Music Archives*

Van Morrison: A Period of Transition, the late 1970s and early 1980s

In 1977 Van entered the Warner Brothers studios after a two and a half year absence to record *A Period of Transition*. This album, co-produced with Mac Rebennack (Dr. John), contained rhythm and blues oriented songs. There were also rock tunes and blues influences reminiscent of Van's earlier music but *A Period of Transition* was not a rock and roll album. It was an extremely commercial collection of songs which owed more to the blues than to rock music. It was obvious that Van intended to recapture his hit-making success in this album. Although *A Period of Transition* remained on the *Billboard* album charts for 11 weeks and eventually peaked at number 43, it was not a strong commercial success. Warner Brothers distributed a beautiful cloth tote bag containing the album, a set of Van Morrison pictures and a book analyzing his career. This elaborate promotion did little to garner airplay and none of the songs from the album made the *Billboard* 45 charts. Surprisingly, in the midst of the album's promotion, in December, 1977 "Moondance" appeared briefly on the *Billboard* 45 charts for four weeks. This was the first time since January, 1973 that Van had a song on the 45 charts.

Van had no apparent concern for the *Billboard* charts. "Basically at heart I am a rocker who no longer wants to be associated in any way with rock and roll music," Van explained. His attitude was a reaction to the "cult status" that many writers used to describe his appeal. "People begin to get a pre-conceived idea about a particular artist," Van suggested, "and that can sometimes work against you." Another influence upon Van was disco music. He found it difficult to believe that this artificially produced and directed music could suddenly engulf the American music scene.

In 1977 Van's music was increasingly performed in small clubs in Marin County. He was often seen shopping with his daughter in Mill Valley or at his parents' record store in Fairfax. Then suddenly Van decided to move to London. He not only believed that a change in musical environment would stimulate his songwriting, but that he would also meet and play with new musicians in the English clubs. In order to promote Van's new musical experiments Warner Brothers set up a series of concerts at Maunkberry's, a fashionable club in the west end of London. The supporting musicians included Mac Rebennack on piano, Mick Ronson on guitar, Mo Foster on bass and Peter Van Hook on drums. During the sets Brian Auger, Peter Bardens and Bobby Tench added their vocal and instrumental talents. To the right of the stage quietly tapping his fingers, Graham Parker sat and watched three nights worth of shows.

However it was not long before Van tired of the English music scene. In 1978 he returned to Mill Valley and signed a management agreement with the Bill Graham organization. Graham placed Nick Clainos in charge of Van's tours. In order to establish a working relationship with Van's road manager and the musicians and friends who toured in his show, a small concert at Mill Valley's Sweetwater Club was arranged. This 150 capacity club is a favorite of local San Francisco performers and a brief mention of the concert over Marin County FM station KTIM resulted in an immediate sellout. This smooth running show set the precedent for a year-long tour.

In October, 1978 Van Morrison began his *Wavelength* tour with three nights of sold-out concerts at Bill Graham's Old Waldorf club in San Francisco. This intimate but acoustically sophisticated club was the perfect warm-up for Van's lengthy tour to promote his new album. Not only was the tour an unqualified success but the *Wavelength* album rose to number 28 on the *Billboard* album charts and remained there for 23 weeks. It was Van's most successful album since *St. Dominic's Preview* but the critics inappropriately hailed it as a "comeback album." There was only one 45 song on the charts as the album's title song, "Wavelength" hit number 42 on a brief stay on the *Billboard* listings. But the songs on the *Wavelength* album were beautifully crafted and the producers of the movie, "An Officer and a Gentleman" bought the rights to "Hungry For Your Love."

One of the most interesting sidelights to the *Wavelength* tour was the decision to tape a live Van Morrison concert for release to radio stations as

Van during the *Wavelength* tour, 1978. *Photo courtesy Don West*

part of the "Warner Brothers Music Show." On November 26, 1978 *Live At The Roxy* was recorded before a select audience. The album was sent to radio stations in January, 1979. As a result of its unique collection of live sounds, Impossible Recordworks quickly issued a bootleg LP, *George Ivan Morrison*. The sound quality on the bootleg was excellent but the outside cover was a xeroxed picture of Van with a listing of songs. However, it does remain as Van's best live album and is a unique collectors' item.

There were also some important musical changes in Van's life. Pee Wee Ellis, James Brown's former musical director, added his talents to Van's band. For years Van had been able to use some of the most creative horn arrangements in music and Ellis helped Van to reach new heights in his use of horns. In 1979 when the *Into the Music* album appeared another positive addition to Van's band was found in Mark Isham's trumpet. The sound that Van had been searching for since 1974 was beginning to take shape as he molded a group of outstanding musicians who provided the most professional backup music of his career. But changes in radio format and the rise of new types of music hindered the album's commercial success. *Into the Music* stayed on the charts for 13 weeks and rose to number 43 on the *Billboard* listings. There was not a chart 45 record from the *Into the Music* album except for a fleeting one week appearance by "Bright Side Of The Road" on the *Billboard* 45 charts.

In addition to the touring there were some interesting events at this time. During the summer of 1979 David Hayes, the bass player with the Jesse Colin Young band, was hired to play a wedding in Marin County. Hayes called his new group "Mechanical Bliss Plus One." As they set up to play on a long green lawn, the lead singer and saxophone player present was Van Morrison. The two hundred guests were oblivious to the treat in store for them that afternoon. As a result of the band's tight structure, Van agreed to play for two nights at the Rancho Nicasio dance hall. During these shows Van covered Ivory Joe Hunter's "Since I Fell For You," and the shows were an outstanding combination of blues and rock music.

When the *Wavelength* tour ended in 1979 Van concluded it with a national broadcast on the King Biscuit Flower Hour show. After Huey Lewis and the American Express opened the show, Van performed for more than an hour. It was a tight and highly emotional set in which Van and his band showed the advantages of a year-long tour. But this was the last Van Morrison tour for some time. He continued to perform in small halls like the Phoenix Theater in Petaluma. On September 7, 1980 Van was forced to play lead guitar when his regular guitarist failed to show and the concert lasted only an hour. He performed nine songs and did two encores. When Van closed the show with his final encore, "Haunts Of Ancient Peace," there were cries for more music.

Van's favorite place to perform recently has been San Francisco's Great American Music Hall. Tom Bradshaw, the manager of this facility, has

Van performing at the Keystone
in Palo Alto, California in 1980.
Photo courtesy Chris Bradford

acted recently as Van's quasi-official manager and the hall is perfectly suited to small crowds. During a March 4, 1981 concert Van politely suggested that a local rock critic, Joel Selvin, had incorrectly labeled his music as rock and roll. Van spoke out on stage that he had worked 15 years to develop a jazz-blues fusion and he implied that Selvin did not understand his music. It was an interesting and thoughtful comment. Selvin, who is a critic for the *San Francisco Chronicle* and teaches a course in the history of rock and roll music at San Francisco State University is quite knowledgeable and aware of the local music scene. His differences with Van about defining Van's music provide an interesting reflection on how difficult it is to agree on Van Morrison's musical direction.

In 1980 the release of the *Common One* album indicated renewed mystical directions were influencing Van's music. Much like Beethoven, Van's music goes to great lengths to avoid following the same patterns. Professor Nathan Rubin of California State University at Hayward toured with Van in 1973 and offered the observation that "Van Morrison had one of the strongest talents for setting up a structure in which something predictable is avoided." Rubin went on to add that Morrison was one of the most creative musicians he had ever encountered at any level. There is a literary quality to the *Common One* album which indicates that Van's reading interests were providing some new insights into his music.

The *Common One* album was the last LP produced under the aegis of Bill Graham's management firm. In 1980 Graham's organization carefully scrutinized the strategy of Journey. One of the main reasons for Journey's continued superstar success was that Herb Herbert, Journey's manager, maintained fresh, hit-making talent in the organization. Herbert pumped new life into Journey with the addition of vocalist Steve Perry and then followed with such carefully selected musicians as Jonathan Cain and Steve Smith. The Graham organization believed that similar additions to Van's band would produce hit-oriented albums.

Nick Clainos' office refuses to comment on the organization of Van's band and no one knows precisely why Bill Graham and Van ended their working relationship. Graham is America's most astute concert producer and his management firm represents only an exclusive group of artists. But Graham is also a shrewd businessman who recognized the recession in the rock business. He believed that musicians like Pee Wee Ellis, Mark Isham and John Allair were the type who would bring Van's music back to popularity on the radio. It is probable that Van resisted any attempts to restructure his music. Whatever the reasons, Van Morrison and Bill Graham parted company in early 1981.

After Van left Bill Graham's management, Jerry Wexler and Ted Templeman were considering an album project for Warner Brothers with Van. However, a story in the San Francisco area rock journal, *BAM*, killed the project. The *BAM* article was an interview with Ted Templeman. During the course of a long and very candid conversation Templeman observed "I really like Van as a person, he's a nice guy, but he's irrational." This interview was an excellent piece of journalism focusing on the various artists produced by this well-known producer. Reflecting on his work with Van, Templeman stated that he would never work with Van again. "He's a marvelous talent, a fantastic singer, but he's fired everyone who ever worked with him; all his producers, his managers, his attorneys, his wives, his kids." In a subsequent issue of *BAM* Templeman attempted to soft pedal these remarks, but they are probably the reason that the Templeman-Jerry Wexler album was not produced for Warner Brothers.

There is no doubt that Van Morrison is a difficult entertainer to interview, but this is often the result of questions asked by rock critics. The field of rock journalism is filled with egomaniacal or starstruck journalists who fail to do their homework and often antagonize the recording artist. This is the primary reason for Van's often uncooperative attitude toward the press. Perhaps the best interview of Van's career took place on a dark, rainy afternoon in the studios of San Francisco's top rated FM rock station, KMEL. In the late afternoon of Friday, November 13, 1981, Van arrived in the KMEL studios to do an interview with Paul Vincent. Unlike many radio personalities, Vincent is a low-key but probing disc jockey who often understates his views. His interviewing techniques are responsible for some of the best live programs on rock radio. In 1980 for example, Vincent talked to Bob Dylan about his career and this interview was circulated widely among Dylan collectors. Vincent, as well as another San Francisco radio personality, Don West, is also one of the most knowledgeable people concerning Van's career. As a result of this interest in lyrical song poets like Dylan and Van Morrison, Vincent was able to ask some of the best questions that Van had ever encountered. The interview produced a number of important insights into Van's career.

During the interview Van related his feelings about his early days in the business. He viewed himself primarily as an artist. However, in the course of the conversation, Van pointed out that he reached a point in the early 1970s where he was forced to consider the business side of his career. When the conversation turned to tours Van suggested: "I started going on the road when I was 15 so by the time I was 21 I had had enough of touring, before I even walked in a studio all I knew was touring."

One of the more surprising points that Paul Vincent was able to draw from Van was tht he did not consider himself a songwriter. "I know songwriters," Van exclaimed, "and I am not one." In Van's view a songwriter was someone who worked a 9 to 5 day. For Van producing music was the result of inspiration. There was also a light side to the interview when Van suggested that "Mechanical Bliss" was an attempt to do a comedy record, and Van pointed out that Dudley Moore loved the record, "but Warner Brothers buried it."

There were also a number of important points not included when the interview was later printed in *BAM* magazine. For example, Van talked for some time about Miles Davis, the music of Little Walter, and the way in

Van at the KMEL interview in San Francisco, 1981. *Photo courtesy Kenny Wardell*

Van and interviewer Paul Vincent at the KMEL studios, November 13, 1981.
Photo courtesy Kenny Wardell

which current artists had developed their material from Van's music. One of the most interesting aspects of the interview was Vincent's ability to draw Van out of his art. "I'm an inspirational writer," Van stated, "I've always got bits and pieces hanging around."

The February 13, 1982 issue of *BAM* also carried an introduction to the edited interview and a discography by Blair Jackson which provided an analytical examination of Van's music. Jackson's comments were perceptive and thoughtful. As Jackson suggested in the introduction, "those who have sought out Van's music in the couple of years since his late AM hit, "Wavelength" know that Van is still growing, still vital." To prove his point, Blair analyzes 14 of Van's albums between 1967 and 1982 and he attempts to provide a roadmap to Van's highly personal musical skills.

Since 1981 Van has increasingly confined his concerts to San Francisco and London. It is quite common for the Van Morrison tour to include two weeks in northern California and two weeks in Europe. One of his favorite spots to perform is the Hardrock Cafe in Copenhagen, Denmark. As one current band member said, "We are never away from home for more than two weeks." This suggests that Van will no longer consider a lengthy tour. He often limits his concerts to the Great American Music Hall or small clubs and auditoriums. The days of performing in huge halls like Pauley Pavilion at UCLA are over for Van Morrison.

Along with his retreat from performing in large auditoriums Van has once again become more mystical in his writing in the 1980s. An example of this trend is *Beautiful Vision*. When this album appeared in 1982 it was in the same vein as *Common One*. There were some new additions to Van's musical lineup, however, as Chris Michie's guitar added new depth to Van's music. Van's albums continued to use guest musicians like Mark Knopfler of Dire Straits who provided support to Michie's lead guitar on two songs, "Cleaning Windows" and "Aryan Mist" on the *Beautiful Vision* album. Michie has also remained an integral part of Van's band. A veteran of the San Francisco music world, Michie began his professional career in 1965 with The Grapes of Wrath. This excellent San Francisco band failed to achieve commercial success and for the next fifteen years Michie played in a number of blues and rock bands. After he was signed by W.E.A. of Holland, he eventually became a member of Van's band. On the *Beautiful Vision* album Michie blends in with the other musicians to create a sense of cohesion and unity.

The *Beautiful Vision* album is an eclectic collection of Van Morrison songs. It included "Cleaning Windows," a Top 40 type song which Warner Brothers released as a 45. The B side was a beautiful instrumental, "Scandinavia." Although this record was intended for AM and FM radio, it failed to make the *Billboard* charts. There were also mystical and experimental songs like "Celtic Ray" which used pipes to set the mood, and "Aryan Mist" which developed spiritual themes similar to those in Bob Dylan's recent music. This album received very little airplay because the Album Oriented Rock (AOR) stations found the songs too long or musically too obtuse.

By 1982 Van was settled into a comfortable, middle class lifestyle. "If anybody looked at the way I live these days—it's so removed from what people think," Van commented. "In fact it's dull and boring. I've got nothing to do with that rock and roll stuff at all." Van went on to say that making music was his vocation, but he had no interest in contemporary pop music. Journey's recent video game is a good example of the excessive commercialization of rock and roll music, but it is highly unlikely that there will ever be a Van Morrison video game.

There is no doubt that Van Morrison's career represents another side to the rock music world. His records are not frequently played on Album Oriented Rock stations because these radio outlets are programmed with well-established current hits. Van's lyrics are too intelligent and mystical for teenaged listeners and the oldies stations prefer "Gloria" and "Here Comes The Night." Yet Van's albums continue to sell well to a wide range of people. He is not a "cult artist" as rock journalists suggest, rather his music appeals to a wide ranging rock, blues and jazz audience. Unlike the music of popular groups like Van Halen, Pat Benatar and Tom Petty, Van Morrison has refused to follow a narrowly defined musical formula. In fact, he strives to avoid predictable, hit-oriented songs, constantly striking out in new directions. Mark Naftalin, a former member of Van's band, summed up his musical genius accurately when he stated, "Van Morrison is capable of inspiring and projecting great musical feeling." Another view of Van's music is that of radio personality Don West, "I trust Van to take me where he wants me to go."

In summarizing Van Morrison's career there are a number of reasons for his tremendous success. Van's unique voice is similar to a saxophone and he has a way of interpreting songs that no other artist possesses. His writing skills are extraordinary as he weaves poetic lyrics and places them into an intriguing musical context. The mystical qualities of Van's music provide an intellectual direction that is generally absent in popular music. The reason that people are still interested in Van's art is because the music continues to hold up. He is a master craftsman in a field dominated by slick writers and popular culture pretenders. The mystic's music is a continual creative force in the current music crisis.

Don West, San Francisco
radio personality,
backstage at the Old
Waldorf during Van's
performance in 1978.

Mark Naftalin, San
Francisco blues artist
and festival-radio
producer. *Photo
courtesy Billy Asprodites*

Taken in an interview with the *Detroit Free Press*, 1974.

Van performing at San Francisco's Palace of Fine Arts, October 21, 1981.
Photo courtesy Don West

Van at the Keystone in Palo Alto, California in 1980. *Photo courtesy Chris Bradford*

II. Miscellany

Van Morrison Chart Songs: 45s in America

Disc No.	Title	Billboard Chart Date	Position	Weeks on Charts
PARROT Chart 45s *(performed with Them)*				
Parrot 9727	Baby Please Don't Go	March 1965	108	8
Parrot 9749	Here Comes The Night	July 1965	24	10
Parrot 9796	Mystic Eyes	Dec. 1965	33	8
Parrot 9727	Gloria	May 1966	71	7
BANG Chart 45s				
Bang 545	Brown-Eyed Girl	Sept. 1967	10	16
Bang 552	Ro Ro Rosey	Nov. 1967	107	2
WARNER BROTHERS Chart 45s				
W.B. 7383	Come Running	April 1970	39	8
W.B. 7434	Domino	Dec. 1970	9	12
W.B. 7462	Blue Money	March 1971	23	12
W.B. 7488	Call Me Up In Dreamland	June 1971	95	2
W.B. 7518	Wild Night	Nov. 1971	28	11
W.B. 7543	Tupelo Honey	Febr. 1972	47	8
W.B. 7573	Straight To Your Heart, Like A Cannonball	April 1972	119	2
W.B. 7616	Jackie Wilson Said	Sept. 1972	61	6
W.B. 7638	Redwood Tree	Nov. 1972	98	2
W.B. 7665	Gypsy	Jan. 1973	119	2
W.B. 8450	Moondance	Dec. 1977	92	4
W.B. 8661	Wavelength	Sept. 1978	42	11
W.B. 49086	Bright Side Of The Road	Nov. 1979	110	1

Van Morrison 45 Discography

THEM: PARROT RECORDS 45s

Parrot 356	Gloria/If You And I Could Be As Two
Parrot 9704	Don't Start Crying Now/One Two Brown Eyes
Parrot 9727	Gloria/Baby Please Don't Go
Parrot 9749	Here Comes The Night/All By Myself
Parrot 9784	I'm Gonna Dress In Black/Half As Much
Parrot 9798	Mystic Eyes/If You And I Could Be As Two
Parrot 9819	Call My Name/Bring 'Em On In
Parrot 3003	Richard Cory/Don't You Know
Parrot 3006	I Can Only Give You Everything/Don't Start Cryin' Now

VAN MORRISON Solo: BANG RECORDS 45s

Bang 545	Brown-Eyed Girl/Goodbye Baby
Bang 552	Ro Ro Rosey/Chick-A-Boom
Bang 585	Spanish Rose/Midnight Special

VAN MORRISON Solo: WARNER BROTHERS 45s

W.B. 7383	Come Running/Crazy Love
W.B. 7434	Domino/Sweet Jannie
W.B. 7462	Blue Money/Sweet Thing
W.B. 7488	Street Choir/Call Me Up In Dreamland
W.B. 7518	Wild Night/When That Evening Sun Goes Down
W.B. 7543	Tupelo Honey/Starting A New Life
W.B. 7573	Like A Cannonball/Old, Old Woodstock
W.B. 7616	Jackie Wilson Said/You've Got The Power
W.B. 7638	Redwood Tree/St. Dominic's Preview
W.B. 7665	St. Dominic's Preview/Gypsy
W.B. 7706	Warm Love/I'll Be There
W.B. 7744	Green/Wild Children
W.B. 7786	Gloria/
W.B. 7797	Ain't Nothin' You Can Do/Wild Children
W.B. 8029	Bulbs/Cul De Sac
W.B. 8411	Joyous Sound/Mechanical Bliss
W.B. 8450	Moondance/A Cold Wind In August
W.B. 8660	Wavelength/Checkin' It Out
W.B. 8743	Natalia/Lifetimes
W.B. 8805	Kingdom Hall/Checkin' It Out
W.B. 49086	Bright Side Of The Road/Rolling Hills

45 Discography Continued

W.B. 49162	Full Force Gale/You Make Me Feel So Free
W.B. 50031	Cleaning Windows/Scandinavia

MISCELLANEOUS 45 RELEASES

Hip Pocket Record 16	3" 45 rpm record	Brown-Eyed Girl/Midnight Special
W.B. Back-to-Back Hits		Moondance/Into The Mystic
W.B. Pro	12" DJ Copies Only	Wavelength (long)/Wavelength
W.B. Pro	12" DJ Copies Only	Natalia/Natalia
W.B. Pro	12" DJ Copies Only	Kingdom Hall/Kingdom Hall
W.B. Pro	12" DJ Copies Only	Bright Side Of The Road/Bright Side Of The Road
W.B. Pro	12" DJ Copies Only	Haunts Of Ancient Peace/Summertime In England

European 45 and Extended Play Album Releases: A Select List for Collectors

THEM-Decca EP 457.073 (France)
Side One: *Gloria/Baby Please Don't Go*
Side Two: *Here Comes The Night/All For Myself*

THEM-Decca 45 F12355 (Spain)
Call My Name/Bring 'Em On In

THEM-Decca EP BU70 500 (Holland)
Side One: *Friday's Child/Baby, What You Want Me To Do*
Side Two: *Stormy Monday/Time's Getting Touger Than Tough*

VAN MORRISON-Pink Elephant Label 45 PE22.541 (Holland)
Spanish Rose/Who Drove The Red Sports Car

VAN MORRISON-Stateside HSS1202 45 (Holland)
Brown-Eyed Girl/Goodbye Baby

VAN MORRISON-Warner Brothers 45 WB7383 (Holland)
Crazy Love/Come Running

European 45s and Extended Play Albums Continued

VAN MORRISON-Warner Brothers 45 WB7488 (Holland)
Call Me Up In Dreamland/Street Choir
VAN MORRISON-Warner Brothers 45 WB16392 (Germany)
Caledonia/What's Up Crazy Pup
VAN MORRISON-Warner Brothers 45 WB16486(N) (Germany)
Bulbs/Who Was That Masked Man
VAN MORRISON-Warner Brothers 45 WB17.254 (Holland)
Wavelength/Checkin' It Out
VAN MORRISON-Mercury 45 60 01 121,2 (Spain)
Bright Side Of The Road/Rolling Hills
VAN MORRISON-Mercury 45 MER99 (England)
Cleaning Windows/All In The Game

Van Morrison Chart Albums in America

Disc No.	Title	Billboard Chart Date	Position	Weeks on Charts
THEM: PARROT RECORDS				
Parrot 61005	Them	July 1965	54	23
Parrot 61008	Them Again	April 1966	138	6
Parrot 71054	Them feat. Van Morrison	July 1972	154	11
VAN MORRISON: BANG RECORDS				
Bang 2189	Blowin' Your Mind	Oct. 1967	182	7
Bang 400	T.B. Sheets	Jan. 1974	181	4
VAN MORRISON: WARNER BROTHERS RECORDS				
W.B. 1835	Moondance	March 1970	29	22
W.B. 1884	His Band and The Street Choir	Dec. 1970	32	17
W.B. 1950	Tupelo Honey	Oct. 1971	27	24
W.B. 2633	St. Dominic's Preview	August 1972	15	28
W.B. 2760	It's Too Late To Stop Now	March 1974	53	17
W.B. 2805	Veedon Fleece	Nov. 1974	53	10
W.B. 2987	A Period of Transition	May 1977	43	11
W.B. 3212	Wavelength	Oct. 1978	28	23
W.B. 3390	Into The Music	Sept. 1979	43	13
W.B. 3462	Common One	Sept. 1980	73	10

Van Morrison Trivia

Cover Versions of Van Morrison Songs

Gloria
The Shadows of Night
Jimi Hendrix
Patti Smith
Bruce Springsteen
Eddie and The Hotrods
Santa Esmeralda

I Wanna Roo You
Dusty Springfield
Goldie Hawn
Jackie DeShannon

I Shall Sing
Art Garfunkle
Miriam Makeba
Toots and The Maytals
Loyal Garner

Wild Night
Martha Reeves and the Vandellas
Amazing Rhythm Aces

He Ain't Give You None
Freddie Scott

T.B. Sheets
John Lee Hooker

Tupelo Honey
Richie Havens

Into The Mystic
Johnny Rivers

I've Been Working
Bob Seger and the
   Silver Bullet Band

Crazy Love
Rita Coolidge
Helen Reddy
Vicki Carr
The Happenings
Esther Phillips

Moondance
Irene Reed
Lorraine Feather
Terry Garthwaite

Brand New Day
Frankie Laine
Miriam Makeba
Esther Phillips
Dorothy Morrison

Brown-Eyed Girl
El Chicano
Ian Matthews
Paul Henry Band

Slim Slow Slider
Johnny Rivers

Bit By Bit
Roy Head

Domino
Buddy Rich

Flamingos Fly
Sammy Hagar

Feedback on Highway 101
Johnny Winter

Jackie Wilson Said
Dexy's Midnight Runners

Films, Television and Concert Recordings featuring Van Morrison's Songs

Welcome To The Fillmore East (NET 1971) - "Cypress Avenue"
Van Morrison At The Rainbow (BBC TV 1971) - various songs
Slipstream (Canada 1974) - "Astral Weeks"
The Last Waltz (USA 1976) - "Caravan" and "Irish Lullaby"
An Officer And A Gentleman (USA 1982) - "Hungry For Your Love"

Other Artists' Influence on Van Morrison

BLUES

John Lee Hooker
Little Walter
Big Joe Williams
Rice Miller (Sonny Boy Williamson)
Jimmy Reed
Sonny Terry and Brownie McGhee
Jelly Roll Morton
Slim Harpo
Bobby Blue Bland
Jesse Fuller
Champion Jack Dupree
Ray Charles
Muddy Waters
Screamin Jay Hawkins

COUNTRY MUSIC

Hank Williams
Big Bill Campbell
Eddie Arnold
Tex Morton
Jimmy Rodgers

JAZZ

Mose Allison
Miles Davis
Sarah Vaughan
Hank Crawford
David "Fathead" Newman

Other Artists' Influence Continued
CONTEMPORARY AUTHORS

Jack Kerouac
J.P. Donleavy
Henry Miller
John Giorno
Alice Bailey
Kurt Vonnegut

Songs and Production With Other Artists

Produced Jackie DeShannon for Atlantic Records 45-2919.

Wrote *Sweet Sixteen* for Jackie DeShannon and played saxophone and provided vocal accompaniment, Atlantic Records 45-2919.

Performed on two John Lee Hooker albums: *Never Get Out Of These Blues Alive* and *Born In Mississippi And Raised In Tennessee.* Songs performed were "Never Get Out Of These Blues Alive" and "Going Down."

Performed and co-wrote "4% Pantomime" on The Band's *Cahoots* album (Capitol 1651).

Performed the lead vocal on Frank Zappa's "Dead Girls Of London." Originally to be released on an *L. Shankar* LP 1979. (Bootleg record version available on Lunar Tunes 2s 5).

Instrumental saxophone break provided on Bill Wyman's solo album, *Stone Alone.*

Performed in The Band's Last Waltz concert at the Fillmore West. Sang "Caravan" and "Irish Lullaby."

Van Morrison Song Titles Changed

Madame Joy became *Madame George.*
Into The Misty became *Into The Mystic.*
Brown Skinned Girl became *Brown-Eyed Girl.*

Some of Van Morrison's Favorite San Francisco Area Bands
Clover
Asleep At The Wheel
Lamb

Van Morrison Bootleg Albums

BELFAST COWBOY (TMOQ 73035)
Recorded at Pacific High Studios, November 1971. Broadcast over
San Francisco radio station KSAN-FM.

SIDE ONE	SIDE TWO
Brown-Eyed Girl	*Ballerina*
Moonshine Whiskey	*Blue Money*
Moondance	*Buenasera Senorita*
Wild Night	

Sound Quality: Excellent stereo reproduction

CHAIR FELLOWS (Impossible Recordworks 1-18)
Recorded at the Bottom Line, New York City, November 1978.

SIDE ONE	SIDE TWO
Moondance	*Kingdom Hall*
Wavelength	*Tupelo Honey*
Into The Mystic	*Wild Night*
Checkin' It Out	*Caravan*
Hungry For Your Love	
Brown-Eyed Girl	

Sound Quality: Excellent stereo reproduction

GEORGE IVAN MORRISON (Impossible Recordworks 1MP1-101)
Recorded at the Roxy Theater, Los Angeles, November 26, 1978.

SIDE ONE	SIDE TWO
Brown-Eyed Girl	*Kingdom Hall*
Wavelength	*Moonshine Whiskey*
Stoned Me	*Help Me*
Checkin' It Out	*Cypress Avenue*
Sweet Thing	

Sound Quality: Excellent stereo reproduction of a Warner Brothers album
sent only to radio stations.

Bootleg Albums Continued
A SPAWN OF THE DUBLIN PUBS (TMOQ)
Recorded at the Troubadour, Los Angeles, May 24 and 27, 1973.

SIDE ONE	SIDE TWO
St. Dominic's Preview	*Domino*
These Dreams Of You	*Warm Love*
The Way Young Lovers Do	*Caravan*
Bad Man Looking For A Fight	*Cypress Avenue*
More And More	
Listen To The Lion	

Sound Quality: Excellent mono sound.

VAN THE MAN (HHCER 109)
Recorded at the Fillmore West, 1970 and Pacific High Studios, October 1971.

SIDE ONE	SIDE TWO
Moondance	*Hound Dog*
Caledonia Soul Music	*Dead Or Alive*
	Friday's Child
	Just Like A Woman

Sound Quality: Excellent mono sound.

VAN MORRISON: THE MYSTIC AND HIS MUSIC, LIVE
Volume 1 (1982)
Recorded at Winterland, San Francisco, October 12, 1979

SIDE ONE	SIDE TWO
Into The Mystic	*Blue Money*
Hound Dog	*Bring It On Home To Me*
Just Like A Woman	*On The Saxophone*
	Buonasera Signorina

Sound Quality: Fair to poor.

Flying Horses Records Ltd., 43 E. 50th Street, New York, New York

72

Best Unreleased Van Morrison Album

Recorded June, 1975 at the Record Plant in Sausalito, California

Songs in Order of Recording:

> *I'm Not Working For You*
> *You Move Me*
> *When I Deliver*
> *I Have Finally Come To Realize*
> *Joyous Sound*
> *Naked In The Jungle*
> *If The Street Only Knew Your Name*

Song Left Off the *Hard Nose The Highway* Album

> *Feedback Out On Highway 101*

Best Live Van Morrison Concert Broadcast Over Radio

A live broadcast from the Bottom Line nightclub in New York City with Peter Wolf of the J. Geils Band as the MC. The date of the broadcast was November 1, 1978. Set in order of songs:

> *Moondance*
> *Wavelength*
> *Into The Mystic*
> *Checkin' It Out*
> *Hungry For Your Love*
> *Brown-Eyed Girl*
> *Crazy Love*
> *Tupelo Honey*
> *Natalia*
> *Help Me*
> *Wild Night*
> *Joyous Sound*
> *Caravan*
> *Cypress Avenue*

Note: A second broadcast from the Bottom Line featured Bill Graham as the host.

Some Inspiration for Van's Songs

A *San Francisco Chronicle* front page picture of a snowfall in San Anselmo.
>   Song produced: *Snow in San Anselmo*

A Reno, Nevada newspaper article on a St. Dominic's church service in Ireland.
>   Song produced: *St. Dominic's Preview*

Cypress Avenue and Belfast surroundings helped to create many songs.
>   Songs produced: *Cypress Avenue and Madame George*

Van's Roadie, Freddie, taking charge of all aspects of Van's life.
>   Song produced: *I Don't Work For You* (unreleased 1975 recording)

An attempt to write a comedy song.
>   Song produced: *Mechanical Bliss*

A Chuck Berry type rock song modeled after *Sweet Little Sixteen*.
>   Song produced: *Sweet Sixteen*

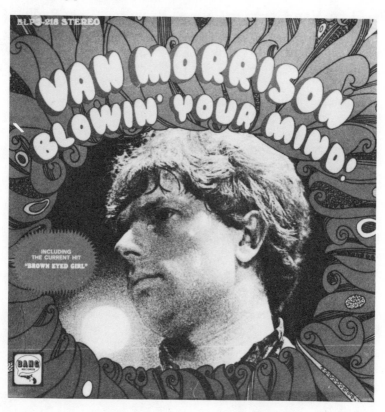

III. Discography

THEM (1965) PARROT 61005 MONO 71005 STEREO
(FEATURING "HERE COMES THE NIGHT")

SIDE ONE

Here Comes The Night (Berns)
Mystic Eyes (Morrison)
Don't Look Back (Hooker)
Little Girl (Morrison)
One Two Brown Eyes (Morrison)
Gloria (Morrison)

SIDE TWO

One More Time (Morrison)
*If You And I Could Be As
Two* (Morrison)
I Like It Like That (Morrison)
I'm Gonna Dress In Black
(Gillon-Howe)
Route 66 (Troup)
Go On Home Baby (Berns)

Prior to this album Them had recorded a song entitled "Don't Start Crying Now" which made little progress in the United Kingdom. But Parrot Records persisted and soon a record release entitled "Baby Please Don't Go" hit the English Pop Charts. This was followed by an appearance on the popular English television show "Ready Steady Go." The flip side of this record was "Gloria" and it soon generated airplay in the United States. The result was that Parrot Records had a hit 45 but no album.

There was also a classic Van Morrison tune on this album, "Mystic Eyes," which Parrot Records failed to promote in the mid-1960s. If Parrot had adequately promoted this song Them's first album would have had three hit records. The conversations among London and Parrot record executives centered on the fear that Them was not a commercially oriented band. As a result Parrot was reticent to record an entire Them album. However, Bert Berns who wrote their first English chart hit, "Baby Please Don't Go," persuaded Parrot to produce an English album entitled, *The Angry Young Them*. It was released in the U.S. as simply *Them*. There is little doubt that Berns' influence and knowledge concerning the recording industry helped Van and the other members of Them. It was Berns' composition "Here Comes The Night" which was highlighted as the album's first hit single. He also wrote "Go On Home Baby." In later years Morrison went on to record for Berns' fledgling label Bang.

SIDE ONE HIGHLIGHTS This side is vintage material from early Van Morrison. On "Here Comes The Night" Van employs a blues infusion interspersed with a staccato vocal style. In 1965 "Here Comes The Night" only reached number 24 on the *Billboard Hot 100*, "Gloria" hit number 93 and "Mystic Eyes" number 33. In one year Van Morrison had three songs on the *Billboard Hot 100* yet he remained an essentially unknown artist. But blues enthusiasts were attracted to Van's blues interpretations. John Lee Hooker's "Don't Look Back" is an excellent example of early blues influences upon Morrison's song styling. A slow, bluesy vocal is backed by a light piano and an almost cocktail lounge drum. The result is one of the finest blues tunes of Morrison's career.

There are two neglected originals on this side of the album. "Little Girl" is a simple, warm paean to a young school mate from Belfast. The structure and tone of "Little Girl" show the influence of Chuck Berry. It demonstrates Van's early rendering of love songs, an approach which would mature in a few years. Another unique song is "One Two Brown Eyes" which contains some interesting guitar licks and a jazz influenced vocal which would soon become Van's musical trademark. There is a tone to this song reminiscent of Bo Diddley, and generally both songs are quite different from early British invasion music or the developing folk rock songs which were becoming popular in 1965. With "Gloria" ending this side, there was little doubt about Van Morrison's credentials as a first-rate rock and roll singer. Almost no one, however, recognized the creative song writing potential or the mystical fusion of blues and jazz which came to dominate his music in the 1970s.

SIDE TWO HIGHLIGHTS The first song, "One More Time," is an indication of the blues influences upon Van's early song styling. He also speaks of making love to a young girl one more time, a theme that runs through much of Morrison's early lyrics. There is a searching, almost yearning desire for a positive, permanent relationship. An eery, poetic recitation begins "If You And I Could Be As Two." This song continues Van's sensitive, youthful search for something to cling to in the plastic world of rock and roll. There is little doubt that this song was directed at the aimless, almost chaotic lifestyle that developed during Them's early years. There has always been a highly moral and family structured tone to Morrison's music and this song reflects those feelings. The final Morrison original on this side is "I Like It Like That" which is mainly a rock and roll song with a blues tone to it.

The three remaining songs are not Van Morrison originals, but he provides some interesting interpretations of other people's work. On "I'm Gonna Dress In Black" there is a tone reminiscent of the early Rolling Stones. On Bobby Troup's "Route 66" Van's vocal styling is greatly influenced by Chuck Berry, but it also adds an uptempo piano and a sense of vocal freedom. The final song, "Go On Home Baby," by Bert Berns also shows the influence of the Rolling Stones, and Van's vocal styling is excellent. John McAuley's harmonica sparkles on this side and there is a soulful note on virtually all of Van's vocals. This is obscure Van Morrison at his best.

SUMMARY This is an excellent example of early Van Morrison. The bluesy vocals are generally interspersed with jazz stylings, and a soulful feeling supports most of the songs. The backup musicians are also excellent. Van's themes of love, relationships and simplicity are very sophisticated at a time when rock music was in a state of transition. It is sad that so few people noticed the quality of Van's song writing. In particular, "Mystic

Eyes" is a good example of in-depth lyrical skill. There is little doubt that the mystic was cutting his teeth on some important themes. As Van told an English reporter: "When I started we were an artsy crowd. Everyone was into creating art through music." This attitude was one which recording executives could not understand, and on Them's second album Van would experience some incredible insights into the cold harsh attitudes of the recording industry. Artistic creation was not as important as hit records and 45 record sales. Van soon faced the choice of continuing the hits of having his recording contract discontinued. He also faced incredible pressures to tour in order to keep the hit records afloat, and these concerts helped to bring Van Morrison to America. As a result of early Them tours Van lived in a number of different American cities and this had an incredible influence upon his music, life and success. Eventually Van would move to New York City, retreat to Boston, flee to Woodstock and settle permanently in Marin County in northern California.

THE ANGRY YOUNG THEM (1965) DECCA LK 4700

SIDE ONE
Mystic Eyes (Morrison)
If You And I Could Be As Two (Morrison)
Little Girl (Morrison)
Just A Little Bit (Gordon)
If I Gave My Love A Diamond (Berns)
Gloria (Morrison)
You Just Can't Win (Morrison)

SIDE TWO
Go On Home Baby (Berns)
Don't Look Back (Hooker)
I Like It Like That (Morrison)
I'm Gonna Dress In Black (Gillon-Howe)
Bright Lights, Big City (Reed)
My Little Baby (Berns-Farrell)
Route 66 (Troup)

Note: This album was reissued by Decca in London in the Pop Legend Series in 1982. (Decca Mono 6835133)

The Angry Young Them is the first English album by Van Morrison's group. The simplistic cover has a beautiful color picture of Them and no writing or other labels. The album has fourteen tracks which include two more songs than the initial Them album issued in the United States.

SIDE ONE HIGHLIGHTS This side has three songs which were not on the American release. "Just A Little Bit," "If I Gave My Love A Diamond," and "You Just Can't Win." The unique interpretation Van applies to these tunes makes this album worthwhile. The remaining songs appeared on the *Them* album issued by London Records' subsidiary label, Parrot, in the United States.

SIDE TWO HIGHLIGHTS   Side two also has three songs which did not
appear on the U.S. album. They are Bert Berns', "Go On Home Baby,"
Jimmy Reed's, "Bright Lights, Big City," and a Berns-Farrell tune, "My
Little Baby."

SUMMARY   This is the first Them album released in England containing
fourteen songs compared to the American release which had only twelve
tunes. It is one of the most collectible Van Morrison records and is enhanced by the album's cover photograph.

THEM AGAIN (1966)   PARROT PAS 710008

SIDE ONE
Could You Would You (Morrison)
Something You Got (Kenner)
Call My Name (Scott)
Turn On Your Lovelight
   (Malone-Scott)
I Can Only Give You Everything
   (Scott-Coulter)
My Lonely Sad Eyes (Morrison)

SIDE TWO
Out Of Sight (Wright)
It's All Over Now Baby Blue
   (Dylan)
Bad Or Good (Morrison)
How Long Baby (Gillon)
Don't You Know (Scott)
Bring 'Em On In (Morrison)

The trials and turmoil of rock and roll music took an unexpectedly heavy
toll upon Them. When the second album was released only Van and one
other original member of the group continued to perform in Them. The
success of "Gloria" and "Here Comes The Night" forced London Records to
record a second album. Since the original members of Them had left the
group, it was only natural to add top session musicians. As a result lead
guitar work was handled by Jimmy Page. Although not listed on the album's liner notes, Page's guitar is a distinct sound throughout the album.
In addition an organ, vibes, flute, and sax are added throughout the album.
This was a musically ambitious set of twelve tunes over which Van had
little control. He has often remarked that Them lived, performed, and died
as a group on the stage of the Maritime Hotel in Belfast. This is an obvious
reference to Van's dislike of the tightly controlled production standards
employed by London Records. Yet, in retrospect, this album stands out as
one of the most exciting rock and roll albums of the mid-1960s.
   When *Them Again* was released in early 1966 few people realized that
this was the end of Van Morrison's experience as a lead singer in a group.
Since Van's writing, arranging, and singing talents overshadowed the rest
of Them it was virtually impossible to contain Van's talent within the
showcase of a group. In many respects this album fits into the mold of the
Yardbirds, Traffic, the Spencer Davis Group, and other blues-influenced
British rock bands that were playing in the mid-1960s.

SIDE ONE HIGHLIGHTS The album opens with a Van Morrison original entitled "Could You Would You." It is a soulful song in which Van communicates in a bluesy style. A catchy organ background and instrumental breaks reminiscent of "Here Comes The Night" add strength and vitality to this cut. "Could You Would You" is essentially a simplistic love song which establishes Van Morrison's ability to communicate clearly with his audience. The personal feeling in his raspy approach to the song adds a special feeling. This is followed by Chris Kenner's "Something You Got." This song was a 1965 hit for Chuck Jackson on Wand Records, and Van eagerly picked up this tune for his second album. The liner notes to this album indicated that Them wanted Tom Scott to write some songs for the album. Whether or not this is true or simply corporate hype is unknown, but Scott's "Call My Name" is a bluesy but fast moving tune which is perfectly suited to Van's vocal stylings. Jimmy Page's guitar solo stands out on this song, and Van is able to present one of his most intimate vocals.

One of the most unique songs on this album is a cover version of Bobby Blue Bland's "Turn On Your Lovelight." Van performs this song with an instrumental precision and he uses a series of backup vocals which provide an extremely effective highlight to his lead vocals. Another Tom Scott song, "I Can Only Give You Everything," is a medium rock and roll number. The final song on this side is Van Morrison's "My Lonely Sad Eyes" which is close to "Here Comes The Night" in instrumental background and vocal stylings.

SIDE TWO HIGHLIGHTS This side opens with a James Brown tune, "Out Of Sight" which Van and his supporting musicians handle with consummate skill. It is an intense and emotional song that crosses over into some of the best blues vocals in Van's early career. This is followed by a version of Bob Dylan's "It's All Over Now Baby Blue" which Greil Marcus considers the first really extraordinary interpretation of a Dylan song by another artist. A Van Morrison original, "Bad Or Good" follows and it is a straight ahead rock and roll number featuring a call and response chorus from a male vocal backup section. These first three songs indicate that Van Morrison was one of the finest pure rock and roll singers of the mid-1960s. A piano solo reminiscent of the 1950s highlights "Bad Or Good," a demonstration of how the roots of early rock music were an in important influence upon his musical style.

In the song "How Long Baby" London Records attempts to use a "Here Comes The Night" type of tune to place Van back on the Top 40 charts. Another Tom Scott song entitled "Don't You Know" is important because of its jazz-oriented direction. The use of a flute and a light instrumental background makes this musical selection quite different from others in the album. The final cut on the album, "Bring 'Em On In," is a Van Morrison original with traces of a Bo Diddley influence. In the 1950s Van listened to a great deal of music from Chicago's Chess Record label and these rhythm and blues and early rock and roll records had an impact upon Van's writing style. This final song is an excellent example of how American rock and roll music influenced the writing and musical styling of young Van Morrison.

SUMMARY This is an album which Van Morrison has often criticized because he lacked the musical controls which characterized his later work. Yet this is an excellent rock and roll collection with jazz and blues overtones. It is also the first time that another artist effectively covered a Bob Dylan song. The mixture of jazz flute and piano is a particularly strong influence on this album, and it suggests some of Van's future musical directions.

THEM AGAIN (1966) DECCA LK 4751

SIDE ONE	SIDE TWO
Could You Would You (Morrison)	*Out Of Sight* (Wright)
Something You Got (Kenner)	*It's All Over Now Baby Blue*
Call My Name (Scott)	(Dylan)
Turn On Your Lovelight	*Bad Or Good* (Morrison)
(Malone-Scott)	*How Long Baby* (Gillon)
I Put A Spell On You (Hawkins)	*Hello Josephine* (Domino-
I Can Only Give You Everything	Bartholomew)
(Scott-Coulter)	*Don't You Know* (Scott)
My Lonely Sad Eyes (Morrison)	*Hey Girl* (Morrison)
I Got A Woman (Charles)	*Bring 'Em On In* (Morrison)

This is the English release of Them's second album on Decca Records. It contains sixteen songs rather than the twelve tunes in the American release. The covers are very similar on each album.

SIDE ONE HIGHLIGHTS "I Put A Spell On You" and "I Got A Woman" are the only two songs on this side that differ from the American album. They are, however, two excellent examples of Van Morrison interpreting the American blues early in his career.

SIDE TWO HIGHLIGHTS The Fats Domino-David Bartholomew composition, "Hello Josephine," and Van's own composition, "Hey Girl" are the only songs on this side which differ from the American release.

SUMMARY The four songs on the English Decca album are a good reason to own both the import and domestic American copy of Them's second album. As with most English Decca products, this is a fine album.

VAN MORRISON: BLOWIN YOUR MIND
(1967) BANG RECORDS BLB 218

SIDE ONE

Brown-Eyed Girl (Morrison)
He Ain't Give You None
   (Morrison)
T.B. Sheets (Morrison)

SIDE TWO

Spanish Rose (Morrison)
Goodbye Baby (Baby Goodbye)
   (Berns-Farrell)
Ro Ro Rosey (Morrison)
Who Drove The Red Sports Car
   (Morrison)
Midnight Special (Berns)

In the midst of the psychedelic revolution in 1967 Bang Records released the *Blowin Your Mind* album with an exploding cover reminiscent of a bad acid trip. Where are you, Owsley, when we really need you? The eight songs included on this album are a strange mix of three-minute would-be hit tunes and long drawn-out pieces like "T.B. Sheets." It was either an album with something for everyone or a rather hastily assembled product. In subsequent interviews Van stated that he was upset not only with the production level, but with the tendency to promote the five three-minute songs. There was little doubt that Bang Records needed some new hits to survive, and this clashed with Van's artistic temperament and his natural aversion to Top 40 hit records.

SIDE ONE HIGHLIGHTS "Brown-Eyed Girl" which became a top ten record and stayed on the charts for sixteen weeks, the longest of any of Van's 45 record releases, is an excellent example of his early hit-making ability. "He Ain't Give You None" is one of Van's most unforgettable early songs, and the nine minute and 44 second version of "T.B. Sheets" is a must for all Van Morrison fans.

SIDE TWO HIGHLIGHTS The eclectic nature of Van's early song writing talents is revealed in "Spanish Rose," a song which is probably an autobiographical song about a girl Van met in New York City shortly after arriving from Ireland. "Goodbye Baby (Baby Goodbye)" is a Bert Berns-Wes Farrell tune written as a two minute and 51 second song designed for the hit charts. It never succeeded, and there was a great deal of dischord between Berns and Van over the song. The next two songs, "Ro Ro Rosey" and "Who Drove The Red Sports Car" appeared on the *T.B. Sheets* album. This side closes with the traditional "Midnight Special," which Bert Berns arranged into a two minute and 45 second song designed for the Top 40 charts.

SUMMARY There is little doubt that Van's comments about this album have hurt its credibility. The disastrous cover design and the fact that only eight songs are included on the album further limits its appeal. Yet there are some positive points to *Blowin Your Mind*. The album contains two interesting songs, "Spanish Rose" and "Midnight Special," which were not previously available to Van Morrison collectors. The fact that five of the eight songs were taken from the *T.B. Sheets* album, however, does limit interest in this release. Despite the fact that it was a rehashing of old Van material, the record is now a collectors item because of the minimal number of copies pressed. For the serious Van Morrison collector, this album is a must for its cover if nothing else.

ASTRAL WEEKS (1968) WARNER BROTHERS 1768

SIDE ONE	SIDE TWO
Astral Weeks (Morrison)	*Young Lovers Do* (Morrison)
Beside You (Morrison)	*Madame George* (Morrison)
Sweet Thing (Morrison)	*Ballerina* (Morrison)
Cyprus Avenue (Morrison)	*Slim Slow Slider* (Morrison)

Astral Weeks is the most important album of Van Morrison's career. Not only did it become an immediate cult favorite, it was instrumental in altering traditional rock and roll musical tastes. Since none of the songs were suitable for AM Top 40 radio play, the album seemed doomed. Its initial sales were extremely weak and most of the major figures in the record industry saw little virtue in *Astral Weeks*. But the advent of FM or underground radio soon made *Astral Weeks* a hit. What eventually became apparent was that Van Morrison was musically and artistically ahead of his time. The musicians who supported Van on the *Astral Weeks* album were able to interpret Van's music in a more sensitive manner than any group of musicians he had worked with in recording sessions. In particular, John Payne's flute and soprano saxophone are important complements to Van's music. Jay Berliner's guitar work and Connie Kay's drumming were also significant ingredients in *Astral Weeks*. The critics remarked that Van's debut album for Warner Brothers combined a jazz-folk tone with dense lyrics. The attempts to interpret *Astral Weeks* are legendary, but Lester Bangs came closest to the truth when he pointed out that Van himself may not have been able to suggest the meaning in all of the songs. This is an album that has different meanings for each listener, and this gives it a special and timeless quality.

SIDE ONE HIGHLIGHTS "Astral Weeks," the title cut is a tour-de-force in sensitive writing. After watching a girl friend die of T.B. and attempting

SIDE TWO HIGHLIGHTS All of the songs on side two except "Joe Harper Saturday Morning" and the vocal and blues-oriented music on this side offers an interesting insight into young Van as a songwriter and storyteller.

SUMMARY This is an excellent album. Although Van was not happy with its release, nevertheless it offers some of his finest early music. The fact that nine of the ten songs are Van Morrison compositions is another important reason for purchasing this album.

MOONDANCE (1970) WARNER BROTHERS 1835

SIDE ONE	SIDE TWO
And It Stoned Me (Morrison)	*Come Running* (Morrison)
Moondance (Morrison)	*These Dreams Of You* (Morrison)
Crazy Love (Morrison)	*Brand New Day* (Morrison)
Caravan (Morrison)	*Everyone* (Morrison)
Into The Mystic (Morrison)	*Glad Tidings* (Morrison)

Moondance was released in February, 1970 on the eve of the announcement that the Beatles were breaking up. It took a month for the album to enter the *Billboard Hot 100*, but it stayed on that chart for 22 weeks. Although *Moondance* reached only number 29 on the *Billboard* charts, nonetheless it established Van Morrison as an artist with a well-defined following. This was important to Warner Brothers executives who were uncertain about Van's future record sales. It is also the first album in which Van had a high degree of personal creative control. Much of the album was recorded in a live setting and all of the arrangements were spontaneous ones. None of the musicians involved in *Astral Weeks* was involved in the *Moondance* album, and this helped to create a fresh approach to Van's music.

SIDE ONE HIGHLIGHTS The leadoff song, "And It Stoned Me," is an intriguing look at Van's view of nature and it also reveals a musical craftsmanship which demonstrates a talent that few people in the record business possess. The presence of Jeff Labes' piano on "And It Stoned Me" provides a beautiful contrast to Van's vocal stylings. The album's title song, "Moondance," offers a jazz-oriented tune which Van intended for pop type singers. "Frank Sinatra wouldn't be out of place singing that," Van remarked. Van used a soprano saxophone while writing "Moondance" and this accounts for its jazz qualities.

   "Crazy Love" is an insightful song about Van's love for Janet Planet, and the sense of stability she provided in his life. "Caravan" was written after Van heard an almost subterranean radio from a neighbor's house in Woodstock. The sense of strong friendship from people like Gypsy Robin and sweet Amarou suggests that this was a happy time in Van's life. Yet "Caravan" also dwells on the mystical ability of a radio to transport itself into Van's house from miles away. This creates the mood for the final song, "Into The Mystic." Originally Van conceived this song as "Into The Misty," but it was changed to "Into The Mystic" largely due to the lyrics. Van suggested that "Into The Mystic" was "about being part of the universe."

SIDE TWO HIGHLIGHTS "Come Running" was the 45 record release from the *Moondance* album, and it was a moderate hit. It remained on the charts for eight weeks and reached number 39 on the *Billboard Hot 100*. "These Dreams Of You" is an extraordinary song written after Van had a dream that Ray Charles was shot down. It is a surrealistic song in which Van provides unique interpretations of his dreams.

"Brand New Day" was written in Boston when Van was in a very down period. Listening to a number of FM radio stations, he was unable to shake negative feelings about the state of rock music. Then a song by The Band came on the radio and Van listened intently. He would eventually live in The Band's hometown, Woodstock, and write a song with Robbie Robertson entitled "4% Pantomime" which appeared on The Band's *Cahoots* album. Van remembered the inspirational song as either The Band's "The Weight" or "I Shall Be Released" and The Band's music served as the inspiration for "Brand New Day."

There is not a mystical quality to "Everyone;" it is simply Van's temporary optimism breaking into song. The album ends with "Glad Tidings" which was a phrase used in a letter that a friend wrote to Van from London. The friend used the term "Glad Tidings" to end his brief message and Van wrote the song to express some of his feelings about his new life in New York City.

SUMMARY *Moondance* is a perfectly crafted album. In fact, many rock critics suggested that it was a collection of songs without a flaw. Since it was the first album Van produced without outside interference, it is a good example of his studio production skills. In particular, he was able to blend many musical talents into an ensemble which seemed to understand his every idea. Van believed that "Brand New Day" was the best song on the album because it indicated a new and positive direction for his life and song writing talents.

HIS BAND AND THE STREET CHOIR (1970)
WARNER BROTHERS 1884

SIDE ONE	SIDE TWO
Domino (Morrison)	*Blue Money* (Morrison)
Crazy Face (Morrison)	*Virgo Clowns* (Morrison)
Give Me A Kiss (Morrison)	*Sweet Jannie* (Morrison)
I've Been Working (Morrison)	*Gypsy Queen* (Morrison)
Call Me Up In Dreamland (Morrison)	*If I Ever Needed Someone* (Morrison)
I'll Be Your Lover, Too (Morrison)	*Street Choir* (Morrison)

This is the most blues-oriented of Van's early albums. There is a tinge of rhythm and blues as well as strong blues vocal stylings which result in two of Van's best blue-eyed soul songs: "Domino," and "Blue Money." Van Morrison's *His Band and the Street Choir* album entered the *Billboard* album charts in December, 1970 and reached number 32 during its 17 week stay on the charts. The hit single, "Domino," was Van's best selling 45 of the 1970s. It rose to number nine on the *Billboard Hot 100* and remained there for three months.

SIDE ONE HIGHLIGHTS "Domino" was probably the most commercial record Van recorded in the 1970s. It blends a straight ahead rock and roll music tone with blues tinges to create a strong, commercially oriented chart song. "Crazy Face" is an allegorical song about freedom and the phrase "I got it from Jesse James" is used to suggest that the man who pulls out the gun sees Jesse James' weapon as a symbol of freedom. The next song, "Give Me A Kiss," is simply a rollicking good-time piece of music. It reflects the simplicity and happiness of Van's life in the early years of his marriage to Janet Planet. The staccato horn section and the jazz influences make this an interesting tune. "I've Been Working" reflects Van's distaste for touring.

"Call Me Up In Dreamland" is one of the strongest songs on the album. The imagery in this song is difficult to interpret but there is a hint of autobiographical feeling. Perhaps Van is reflecting upon his own career when he asks: "Call me up in Dreamland, Radio to the man, Get the message to me, Any way you can..." This side closes with a poignant love song, "I'll Be Your Lover, Too." This is one of the most sensitive songs on the album, and is simply a statement of Van's romantic feelings.

SIDE TWO HIGHLIGHTS "Blue Money" was Van's third best selling Top 40 song in the 1970s. It only reached number 23 on the *Billboard Hot*

100, but it remained on the charts for three months. "Blue Money" had all the requisite musical and lyrical components for a hit record. It was a rollicking, good-time song with a snappy lyrical approach. "Virgo Clowns" helps to balance the more rock-oriented songs on this album by the acoustic lead guitar. This is another love song in which Van intones "let your laughter fill the room." In "Sweet Jannie" Van writes about moonlight walks with Janet Planet and the depth of Van's feeling is demonstrated when he suggests "don't stop walking, till we get to the preacher man." "Gypsy Queen" is in many respects a tribute to Curtis Mayfield and the Impressions. The background and the general tone of the song is reminiscent of the Impressions, but Van gives this unique song his own special twist. "If I Ever Needed Someone" is another blues-oriented song about the problems of convincing a young girl to come out for the night. The backup vocals by Emily Houston, Judy Clay, and Jackie Verdell are the reason that this song works so well. The final song, "Street Choir," is another blues number with strong feeling and a romantic message. It is ironic that many rock critics called this side of the album a weak one, because most of the songs are written with a deep feeling and the musical arrangements are very tight.

SUMMARY   This was a highly commercial album which yielded two substantial hits. However, many of the best songs were ignored by the rock and roll press. Van originally envisioned this album as an a cappella work. Somewhere along the line Warner Brothers gained more control of the album than Van believed was healthy, and he has been very critical of it. Yet *His Band and the Street Choir* remains one of Van's best efforts.

TUPELO HONEY (1971)   WARNER BROTHERS 1950

SIDE ONE	SIDE TWO
Wild Night (Morrison)	*Tupelo Honey* (Morrison)
(Straight To Your Heart) Like A Cannonball (Morrison)	*I Wanna Roo You* (Morrison)
Old Old Woodstock (Morrison)	*When That Evening Sun Goes Down* (Morrison)
Starting A New Life (Morrison)	*Moonshine Whiskey* (Morrison)
You're My Woman (Morrison)	

The marital bliss in Van Morrison's life is reflected in the *Tupelo Honey* album. An innovative producer, Ted Templeman, and a series of excellent new musicians provided the impetus to make this album the happiest in Van's musical repertoire. The initial idea for *Tupelo Honey* was to create a country and western album but the songs were never fully developed in this vein. As a result the *Tupelo Honey* album reflected Van's move to California. In December, 1971 Van's lease on his Woodstock house expired and he moved to his wife's former home, Marin County, in northern California. This change in location made it possible to bring new musicians like Ronnie Montrose in to work on *Tupelo Honey*. Ted Templeman provided the professional production skills which often eluded Van in his earlier work, and the result was a beautifully mixed and edited album. Van called it a "bunch of songs left over from previous sessions," but this ignores the album's numerous strengths. One of the most significant reasons for the musical quality on this piece of work is the drumming of former Modern Jazz Quartet member Connie Kay, the sax playing of Jack Schroer and the work of musicians like Rick Schlosser, Mark Jordan, Luis Gasca, and John McFee. Although Van disliked the album, it is one of his best efforts. *Tupelo Honey* entered the *Billboard* album charts in October, 1971 and spent 24 weeks before peaking at the number 27 position. "Wild Night" spent 11 weeks on the *Billboard Top 100* charts, and "Tupelo Honey" reached number 47 in its eight weeks on the charts.

SIDE ONE HIGHLIGHTS "Wild Night" is one of Van's strongest rock and roll songs. For a singer-songwriter who doesn't consider himself a rock artist, Van has an extraordinary ability to write rock-oriented tunes. In fact, there is almost a bar band sound to most of the songs on this side. "(Straight To Your Heart) Like A Cannonball" is a simple love song with a roadhouse musical backdrop. It is predictable but musically very commercial.

"Old Old Woodstock" is a beautiful tribute to Van's life in upstate New York. Van evokes the feeling of this sleepy New York community when he writes "feeling the breezes blowing around your coat." He also recalls the pastoral tone and the strong sensitivity toward children and family. It is a moving and compelling look at a satisfying period in Van's life. "Starting A New Life" displays the exuberance and joy of moving to Marin County in northern California. "When I hear that robin's song, I know it won't be long," is a line Van uses to celebrate the move to his new home. It is a moment of rediscovery for nature, which was always a part of Van's song writing personality.

This side closes with "You're My Sunshine" which is a slow, bluesy tribute to Janet Planet. Van's deep feelings over the birth of his child and his strong commitment to Janet make the phrase "You are my sunshine" a special one in the song.

SIDE TWO HIGHLIGHTS "Tupelo Honey" is an example of Van's song writing at its best. He is able to paint a picture of Janet Planet's impact on his life. "I Wanna Roo You" recalls Van's Irish past, and it is an excellent song picture of tenderness in a rural, rustic setting. "When That Evening Sun Goes Down" is another straight ahead reflection on the new found serenity of Van's life. The album ends with "Moonshine Whiskey" which is another fun tune without pretension. In fact, this entire side is made up of some of the most understandable and accessible music of Van's career. There is a honky tonk, bar room feeling to this album.

SUMMARY This is one of Van's best albums. It was also an immense commercial success as it sold more than 350,000 copies by June, 1974. The music is simple, direct and full of happiness. There is little mystery and the musical arrangements are some of the best of Van's career. Ronnie Montrose's beautiful guitar work would make heavy metal fans sit up in amazement.

SAINT DOMINIC'S PREVIEW (1972)
WARNER BROTHERS 2633

SIDE ONE
Jackie Wilson Said (I'm In Heaven When You Smile) (Morrison)
Gypsy (Morrison)
I Will Be There (Morrison)
Listen To The Lion (Morrison)

SIDE TWO
Saint Dominic's Preview (Morrison)
Redwood Tree (Morrison)
Almost Independence Day (Morrison)

Although this was Van's fifth album for Warner Brothers he felt that it was a follow-up to *Moondance*. Neither *His Band And The Street Choir* nor *Tupelo Honey* were albums which pleased Van. When *Saint Dominic's Preview* was released in July, 1972 it produced only moderate chart success. "Jackie Wilson Said" was number 61 on the *Billboard Hot 100* and "Redwood Tree" reached number 98. But this is a musically innovative album and the presence of a moog synthesizer indicates a new direction in Van's music. The album also introduces a new musical backup group known as the Caledonia Soul Orchestra which featured important new musicians like Mark Naftalin, a keyboardist with the Paul Butterfield Blues Band, Jules Broussard, a San Francisco jazzman, and Ron Elliot, a member of San Francisco's legendary Beau Brummels.

There was a decided blues-jazz fusion to *Saint Dominic's Preview*. In fact, many of the early 1970s counterculture Van Morrison fans wrote letters to Warner Brothers asking for a return to the good-time music. Ironically, Van would perform very few of the songs from this album. By 1974 only "Listen To The Lion" and "Saint Dominic's Preview" were performed by Van in concerts around the San Francisco area.

SIDE ONE HIGHLIGHTS "Jackie Wilson Said" was one of the more adventurous songs in Van's career. It was a drastic departure from Van's previous music and it reflected the vocal influences of 1950s soul singer Jackie Wilson. Van claimed that Wilson's string of hits were important musical influences because Wilson's interpretations were used in developing Van's early vocal stylings. "Gypsy" is another unique song with acoustic guitar lines in the midst of a powerful instrumental background.

"I Will Be There" is a fine example of a basic blues number reminiscent of a Kansas City blues shouter like Big Joe Turner. "Listen To The Lion" contains some outstanding guitar work by Ronnie Montrose.

SIDE TWO HIGHLIGHTS   "Saint Dominic's Preview" is a song inspired by San Francisco's church of the same name. It is a largely autobiographical song which talks about the long way from Buffalo and Belfast and reflects on life in San Francisco. Van skillfully paints images of the impersonal nature of Safeway supermarkets, and follows this with comments on "not feeling anyone else's pain." "Redwood Trees" is another innovative song which beautifully brings together Van's old life in Ireland with his new found California freedom. The final song, "Almost Independence Day," is another experimental song as Bernie Krause provides some eerie moog synthesizer sounds. Krause was the driving force behind the Byrds' "Space Odyssey." Mark Naftalin provides some excellent piano sounds and also doubles on the moog.

SUMMARY   This album was a major experimental turning point for Van Morrison. Not only was he becoming more mystical, but he was willing to move boldly into new musical directions. Ted Templeman's production techniques brought out another side of Van Morrison, but the strain began to show upon Templeman. In later years he would vow never to work with Van again because he was much too difficult to please. Perhaps Templeman didn't realize that this was the nature of Van's genius.

THEM FEATURING VAN MORRISON
LEAD SINGER (1972)   PARROT BP 71054

SIDE ONE
Could You Would You (Morrison)
Something You Got (Kenner)
Turn On Your Lovelight
    (Malone-Scott)
I Can Only Give You Everything
    (Scott-Coulter)
My Lonely Sad Eyes (Morrison)

SIDE TWO
Out Of Sight (Wright)
It's All Over Now Baby Blue
    (Dylan)
Bad Or Good (Morrison)
How Long Baby (Gillon)
Bring 'Em On In (Morrison)

SIDE THREE
Gloria (Morrison)
Here Comes The Night (Berns)
Mystic Eyes (Morrison)
Don't Look Back (Hooker)
Little Girl (Morrison)

SIDE FOUR
One More Time (Morrison)
If You And I Could Be As
    Two (Morrison)
I Like It Like That (Morrison)
One Two Brown Eyes (Morrison)
Route 66 (Troup)

This is a repackaging of Them songs which the London subsidiary Parrot Records issued in 1972 to capitalize upon Van's enormous popularity. The liner notes by Lester Bangs occupy two full pages inside a foldout cover. The album cover is beautifully produced with a brown simulated leather design. Inside the cover is a small photo of Them. All the songs on this compilation package are taken from the first two Them albums. When the package was assembled, Parrot decided to exclude four songs which had appeared on Them's first two albums.

SIDE ONE HIGHLIGHTS The songs on this side were included as side one on the *Them Again* album, except that Tom Scott's "Call My Name" was left off.

SIDE TWO HIGHLIGHTS This side is made up of side two of the *Them Again* album, but another Tom Scott tune, "Don't You Know," is missing.

SIDE THREE HIGHLIGHTS On the "Here Comes The Night" version of the initial *Them* album that tune was the lead-off song. But Parrot repackaged it and made "Gloria" the lead-off song on the same album. The Them arrangement of that "Gloria" version on the *Them* album is followed here on side three, with one exception. "One Two Brown Eyes" is held over to be used on side four.

SIDE FOUR HIGHLIGHTS This side consists of four songs from side two of the first *Them* album, two songs, "I'm Gonna Dress In Black" and "Go On Home Baby," were deleted from this side and "One Two Brown Eyes" was added to complete the tracks.

SUMMARY This is an excellent compilation of the first two Them albums. It provides twenty of the first twenty-four songs which Them released in the United States. The copious liner notes and the attractive cover make this a worthwhile addition to any Van Morrison collection.

T.B. SHEETS (1973) BANG RECORDS 400

SIDE ONE	SIDE TWO
He Ain't Give You None (Morrison)	T.B. Sheets (Morrison)
Beside You (Morrison)	Who Drive The Red Sports Car? (Morrison)
It's All Right (Morrison)	Ro Ro Rosey (Morrison)
Madame George (Morrison)	Brown-Eyed Girl (Morrison)

The majority of the material on *T.B. Sheets* is compiled from recordings made in 1967. Later tracks were added and a number of these were previously unreleased. The album was generally considered to be an attempt to capitalize upon Van's hit-making abilities in the early 1970s. To no one's surprise Van denounced the album as one which did not do his music justice. This criticism was a trifle harsh, as the album contains a number of important Van Morrison songs. The liner notes by Michael Ochs are the best of any to appear on Van's albums. The album cover is set off with an excellent drawing of Van sitting in an oversized stuffed chair playing an acoustic guitar. The album opens up to reveal a picture of Van tugging on his sport coat. On the opposite page the words to the album's songs are artistically displayed. Over all, the album concept is carried out very nicely.

SIDE ONE HIGHLIGHTS The songs on this side are all Van Morrison originals written in 1967 and 1968, and they are more oriented toward the blues than rock and roll. "He Ain't Give You None" is an interesting tale of Van's infatuation with a young girl in London. It is followed by a 1968 composition, "Beside You," which has surrealistic images in it. The lyrics are reminiscent of Bob Dylan and the tale is an allegorical look at the wanderings of a young child. A 1970 song, "It's All Right," is a slow, bluesy number which again owes a great deal to Dylanesque lyrics. It is a poignant love song which helps to illuminate Van's feelings about a recent love affair.

The most intriguing song on this side is the 1968 tune, "Madame George." Although many think the song to be about a transvestite, Van has denied this for years. The song is set on Cypress Avenue in Belfast, which Van described to a *Rolling Stone* reporter as: "a pretty real place." The song's glimpse into another lifestyle and a different way of thinking makes it an intriguing and poetic piece.

SIDE TWO HIGHLIGHTS "T.B. Sheets" opens this side and it is a classic example of Van's ability to turn a personal experience into a provocative song. While living in Boston he witnessed the death of a girl he lived with in the 1960s. The images of suffering and eventual death are powerfully demonstrated in the lyrics, and the music casts an eerie feeling throughout the song. In the midst of the psychedelic revolution during the "Summer of Love" in San Francisco's Haight-Ashbury, almost no radio station in America was interested in playing a song about death via tuberculosis. Yet, in retrospect, this emotional tune is a vivid example of Van's incredible songwriting and musical skills.

"Who Drove The Red Sports Car?" is one of Van's strangest songs because it sounds like a novelty tune. However, it is again reminiscent of Bob Dylan's music and the lyrics suggest another personal story. "Ro Ro Rosey" is an uptempo composition which traces the story of a sweet young sixteen year old girl. This may be Van Morrison's version of Chuck Berry's "Sweet Little Sixteen." The final song, "Brown-Eyed Girl," was a magic moment for Van in 1967. It was one of Van's best efforts and it was a strong FM radio favorite. Some AM stations censored the song because of the line "making love in the green grass."

SUMMARY This is an important Van Morrison album. Not only is the cover well done, but the lyrics are beautifully set off inside the fold-open cover. Many rock critics have complained about the mundane nature of songs like "Who Drove The Red Sports Car?" However, this ignores Van's ability to take a seemingly innocuous song and translate it into a blues idiom with Dylanesque lyrical strength.

HARD NOSE THE HIGHWAY (1973)
WARNER BROTHERS BS 2712

SIDE ONE	SIDE TWO
Snow In San Anselmo (Morrison)	Green (Raposo)
Warm Love (Morrison)	Autumn Song (Morrison
Hard Nose The Highway	Purple Heather (trad. arrangemt.
(Morrison)	Van Morrison)
Wild Children (Morrison)	
(The Great Deception) (Morrison)	

This album was recorded in 1973 at Van's own recording studio shortly after his parents moved to Fairfax, California from Ireland. Jackie DeShannon sang backup vocals on two songs, "Warm Love," and "Hard Nose The Highway," and Van recorded a song sung by Kermit the Frog on Sesame Street. "Green" was the first non-original song Van recorded since signing with Warner Brothers records. One of the most interesting aspects of this album was Van's decision to use the Oakland Symphony Chamber Chorus as the backing vocals on "Snow in San Anselmo." This song was written after Van read a front page story in the San Francisco Chronicle which also included a page-long picture of a freak snowfall in Marin County. There is a decidedly jazz tone to this album, and the songs are more tightly structured than those on Saint Dominic's Preview. The term "hard nose" is an Irish slang expression which means that a person is unhappy with something.

SIDE ONE HIGHLIGHTS "Snow in San Anselmo" is an unusual song written during a once in a lifetime snowstorm in northern California. The song's images include a pancake house, a massage parlor and a sleepy California town, and they are lyrically tied to the fact that it had not snowed in San Anselmo since World War II. "Warm Love" is a typical Van Morrison love song replete with images of youthful joy. "Hard Nose The Highway" makes three statements about Van's life. First, there is an allusion to Frank Sinatra walking into a recording studio and telling Nelson Riddle to begin the recording session. After completing the album Frank Sinatra takes a vacation, and here Van was alluding to his plans to take a two and a half year break from the music industry. Second, there were complaints about the growing number of musicians who had found a home in Marin County. There is a strange reference to a now defunct Marin dance hall operated by the Grateful Dead. Pepperland was a late 1960s communal dance emporium bankrolled by the Grateful Dead and Van coyly writes, "I was tore down at the dead's place. Shaved head at the organ. But that wasn't half as bad as it was oh no, Belfast and Boston." This was Van's way of letting the hip community in California know that he had been through not only more interesting musical scenes, but ones which were decidely more dangerous. Third, Van complains about the record companies, the promoters and the frenetic grasping for money in the music business.

A slow jazz-based tune, "Wild Children," begins with references to Van's date of birth. The song uses images of James Dean, Marlon Brando and Rod Steiger to recall Van's formative years. This is an intriguing look at one artist's view of growing up in the post-World War II era. The artistic side of Van is shown when he intones: "Tennessee Tennessee Williams, Let your inspiration flow..." The final song, "The Great Deception," was about an encounter that Van had with a liberal-radical type who approached him for money. Van called the song one that he had written for all the hip phonies who hung out on the edges of the rock and roll cultural scene.

SIDE TWO HIGHLIGHTS   "Green" is generally remembered as the song that Kermit the Frog sang on Sesame Street. However, Van had another meaning for this tune, and he identified it as an Irish song. The underlying humility of the lyrics performed by Kermit appeared to touch Van's emotions. The critics were unable to analyze the reason Van recorded the song, and this suggests that the song-poet is often not permitted the slightest frivolity.

"Autumn Song" is a ten minute and 37 second ode to the fall. It is an example of the tremendously creative musical skills which Van Morrison possesses. This song was written as he observed the gradual change in seasons in northern California in the early 1970s. There is also an important sub-theme in "Autumn Song" as Van celebrates his return to Fairfax for the Christmas holidays.

The last tune, "Purple Heather," is Van's arrangement of an old traditional song, "Wild Mountain Thyme," which Van had seen the McPeakes perform in Belfast in the 1950s. Since this was the first album in which Van believed that he had complete control and artistic freedom, it is not surprising that he ended the album with a traditional song.

SUMMARY   This is an excellent album because the songs reveal a great deal about Van's past and future. There is a hint of dissatisfaction with the rock and roll world which is apparent in Van's departure from rock and roll since the mid-1970s. The emotional and creative edge of this album is best represented in "Snow in San Anselmo" and "Hard Nose The Highway." This album is strictly for Van Morrison aficionados and it contains some of his most personal music.

IT'S TOO LATE TO STOP NOW (1974)
WARNER BROTHERS 2 BS-2760

SIDE ONE
Ain't Nothin' You Can Do
(Malone)
Warm Love (Morrison)
Into The Mystic (Morrison)
These Dreams Of You (Morrison)
I Believe To My Soul (Charles)

SIDE TWO
I've Been Workin' (Morrison)
Help Me (Williamson)
Wild Child (Morrison)
Domino (Morrison)
I Just Wanna Make Love To You
(Dixon)

SIDE THREE
Bring It On Home (Cooke)
Saint Dominic's Preview
(Morrison)
Take Your Hand Out Of My Pocket
(Williamson)
Listen To The Lion (Morrison)

SIDE FOUR
Here Comes The Night (Berns)
Gloria (Morrison)
Caravan (Morrison)
Cypress Avenue (Morrison)

It's Too Late To Stop Now is the first live album recorded by Van Morrison. The music was assembled from concerts at Doug Weston's Troubadour Club in Los Angeles, the Santa Monia Civic Auditorium and the Rainbow Theater in London. These live shows were taped in the summer of 1973 and the Caledonia Soul Orchestra provided the musical background. Of the eighteen songs recorded for the album six were blues or rock and roll tunes written by other artists. One Bert Berns composition, "Here Comes The Night," was also included in this excellent retrospective look at Van's career. The reason for this record's release is Van's belief that Them had never been properly recorded in a live show, thereby preventing the public from realizing their fullest musical potential. This thought gnawed away at Van for years and finally the double album was made in an attempt to distill ten years of touring, recording and perfecting his musical skills.

SIDE ONE HIGHLIGHTS "I Believe To My Soul" is the best track on this side. Ray Charles' composition is handled in a straightforward manner similar to the way he performed it in the late 1950s. Other interesting live versions of traditional Van Morrison songs are "Into The Mystic" and "Warm Love."

SIDE TWO HIGHLIGHTS The Sonny Boy Williamson classic, "Help Me," and Willie Dixon's "I Just Wanna Make Love To You" are examples of the skill which Van has always displayed in covering blues tunes. "Domino" is the best live Van Morrison composition on this side.

96

SIDE THREE HIGHLIGHTS Sam Cooke's "Bring It On Home" opens this side and is complemented nicely by Sonny Boy Williamson's "Take Your Hand Out Of My Pocket." "Listen To The Lion" and "Saint Dominic's Preview" are songs which demonstrate Van's ability to perform his hit records superbly in a live setting.

SIDE FOUR HIGHLIGHTS This side is the perfect vehicle to close a live album. "Gloria" and "Here Comes The Night" recall Van's early days in a highly emotional performance. This is followed by the more creative "Caravan" and "Cypress Avenue." What a beautiful way to blend the early part of Van Morrison's career with the later parts which offer more significant original songs.

SUMMARY This is an excellent live album. The songs are not only carefully selected, but the Caledonia Soul Orchestra is a musically creative force anticipating Van's every musical direction.

VEEDON FLEECE (1974) WARNER BROTHERS BS 2805

SIDE ONE	SIDE TWO
Fair Play (Morrison)	*Bulbs* (Morrison)
Linden Arden Stole The Highlights (Morrison)	*Cul De Sac* (Morrison)
Who Was That Masked Man (Morrison)	*Comfort You* (Morrison)
Streets Of Arklow (Morrison)	*Come Here My Love* (Morrison)
You Don't Pull No Punches, But You Don't Push The River (Morrison)	*Country Fair* (Morrison)

After disbanding the Caledonia Soul Orchestra, Van recorded *Veedon Fleece* with a group of musicians who sounded like they had been playing in the Velvet Turtle restaurant in San Rafael. It is lyrically and musically haunting, and the songs are difficult ones to interpret. This album combines much of Van's feelings concerning the breakup of his marriage to Janet Planet with images of his Irish youth.

SIDE ONE HIGHLIGHTS *Veedon Fleece* opens with "Fair Play" which has a plaintive tone and laments growing up in a world full of pressures. It is obvious that some lines from the 1971 tune, "Call Me Up In Dreamland," appear in this song and perhaps remind Van of more pleasurable moments. "Linden Arden Stole The Highlights" is probably the tale of a former Belfast friend of Van's. This song is replete with images of a typical Irish roustabout. The next song performed in a falsetto voice, "Who Was That Masked Man," is a drastic musical departure. A dominating flute solo by Jim Rothermel, who often plays with the Jesse Colin Young band, is an intriguing part of "Streets of Arklow." This song recalls the freedom of a small town or street in Van's past. The final tune, "You Don't Pull No Punches, But You Don't Push The River," is an enigmatic exercise in song writing.

SIDE TWO HIGHLIGHTS   "Bulbs" is a song with baseball imagery, but it suggests that being a musical performer is often all show business. "Cul De Sac" is a reflection on life in a typical California suburb. Van seems to suggest that the cul de sac is an indication of Californians striving for status. He ridicules the beautiful homes and status-oriented lives.

In "Comfort You" Van intones that "you put the weight on me..." This appears to be a comment on the pressures of marriage and a family which may have contributed to his marital breakup. He then weaves a lyrical song pattern which suggests that Van will place the weight on his partner. There is an interesting allegorical tone to this song. "Come Here My Love" is a plaintive love song and is typical of some of Van's early 1970 compositions. "Country Fair" is a beautiful song describing his mellow feelings while attending a fair.

SUMMARY   This is an excellent album. It is probably the most romantic of Van's song writing ventures in the early and mid-1970s. The musical background is enhanced by the Oakland Symphony's Nathin Rubin and the soprano saxophone of Jack Shroer. This is quite a musical departure for Van Morrison but a very satisfying one for the listener.

BACKTRACKIN: THEM FEATURING VAN MORRISON LEAD SINGER (1974)
LONDON RECORDS PS 639

SIDE ONE	SIDE TWO
Richard Cory (Simon)	*Baby Please Don't Go* (Williams)
I Put A Spell On You (Hawkins)	*Hey Girl* (Morrison)
Just A Little Bit (Thornton-Washington-Bass-Brown)	*Don't Start Crying Now* (Moore-West)
If I Gave My Love A Diamond (Berns)	*All For Myself* (Morrison)
Half As Much (Berns)	*Mighty Like A Rose* (Morrison)

This is an American released repackaging with a nice picture of Them from the mid-1960s. It was issued in 1974 to capitalize on Van's enormous popularity, and the small number of albums pressed makes it a definite collector's item. Some of the songs are available on other albums but Van Morrison compositions like "All For Myself," "Mighty Like A Rose," and "Hey Girl" make this album a worthy addition to any collection.

SIDE ONE HIGHLIGHTS Although available on a number of other records, "Richard Cory," "I Put A Spell On You," and "Half As Much" are all interesting songs. "Just A Little Bit" is a fairly rare and interesting song and it is the highlight of side one.

SIDE TWO HIGHLIGHTS This side is interesting because "Baby Please Don't Go," which went to number 10 on the British charts in 1965, is the lead-off song. The sound quality is excellent and the songs provide some interesting insights into Van's early musical development.

SUMMARY This is a collectible album because it was printed in rather small quantities. The music provides a varied look at early Van Morrison, and a number of the songs are difficult to find on American albums. An interesting album and a must for the serious collector. This is because some of the songs were taken directly from the first album released in England on Decca, *The Angry Young Them.*

Rock Roots: THEM (1976)   DECCA ROOTS 3

SIDE ONE	SIDE TWO
Don't Start Crying Now (Moore-West)	*The Story Of Them, Parts 1 and 2* (Morrison)
I'm Gonna Dress In Black (Gillon)	*Mighty Like A Rose* (Morrison)
Route 66 (Troup)	*Times Getting Tougher Than Tough* (Witherspoon)
How Long Baby (Gillon)	
Bright Lights, Big City (Reed)	*Stormy Monday* (Walker)
Don't You Know (Scott)	*Baby What You Want Me To Do* (Reed)
Call My Name (Scott)	*Friday's Child* (Morrison)

Historically, this is an important album. The English Decca people have reissued Them's earliest and rarest tracks. The songs include Them's first important record release, "Don't Start Crying Now," which was issued on September 4, 1964. There are also five songs issued from the 1965-1966 period, and a single release of "The Story Of Them, Parts 1 and 2" which was originally issued as a Dutch single in 1968. There are five tracks not previously issued in the United Kingdom. The liner notes and the album cover are well done, and the overall sound quality is outstanding. This is a record which is very important in analyzing the early blues roots of Van Morrison and Them.

SIDE ONE HIGHLIGHTS There is little doubt that English Decca initially attempted to copy the popularity of the Rolling Stones. The vocal emphasis on "Don't Start Crying Now" and the early publicity surrounding Them epitomized the "bad boys" approach to rock and roll music. Decca's publicity emphasized the scruffy and rebellious nature of Them. This only helped to sour Van Morrison on the recording industry, and he often attempted to counter the inane publicity generated by Decca. Yet for all the fluff and public relations hoopla, "Don't Start Crying Now" has a Mick Jagger type vocal, and the music reflects the blues heritage of bands who were part of the early English invasion. Van repeatedly stated that Them was not a British band, but this song is very typical of the Animals or the Rolling Stones in the early years of the English rock and roll renaissance.

In fact, the next song, "I'm Gonna Dress In Black," is an Eric Burdon inspired vocal with instrumental backing similar to the Animals' sound. This song was originally issued on August 27, 1965 and it was the B side of "It Won't Hurt Half As Much." "Route 66" was on the first Them album but this cut is eight seconds longer than the original. "How Long Baby" was taken from the *Them Again* album and it is a slow, bluesy tune with some beautiful solo guitar work. "How Long Baby" was originally issued as the B side to "One More Time" on June 11, 1965. Van's cover of Jimmy Reed's "Bright Lights, Big City" was issued on the English release of Them's first album, but it was not on the American version. It is a unique rendition of Reed's song, and amply demonstrates Van's early ability to evoke his own blues interpretations. The Tom Scott tune "Don't You Know" is beautifully performed with a jazz-like flute in the background. This song was the B side of "Richard Cory" and was released on May 13, 1966. It appeared on the *Them Again* album. Another Tom Scott song, "Call My Name," also from the *Them Again* album closes this side.

SIDE TWO HIGHLIGHTS "The Story Of Them, Parts 1 and 2" is a seven minute, thirteen second version of this early Them song which was released as a Dutch single in 1968. In the London Collector Series "The Story Of Them, Parts 1 and 2" is a seven minute and 28 second version, and it is interesting to compare the two songs. They appear to be the same song, but one is an alternate cut. The next five tracks are very unique because the songs have not been available in England. One tune, "Mighty Like A Rose," which is a Van Morrison original was not previously available in either the U.S. or the U.K. The remaining songs were never released in the United Kingdom but they have been available on American albums. In 1977 London Records issued *The Story of Them* and the last four songs on this side were included on that album.

SUMMARY This is a visually pleasing and musically sound addition to the Van Morrison archives. Some of the cuts are slightly different than those released on previous albums. The liner notes by Chris Poole are brief but highly informative, and this album provides an interesting look at some obscure Them and Van Morrison musical selections.

THE STORY OF THEM: THEM FEATURING VAN MORRISON LEAD SINGER (1977)
LONDON 50001

SIDE ONE	SIDE TWO
The Story Of Them, Parts 1 and 2 (Morrison)	*Bright Lights, Big City* (Reed)
Times Getting Tougher Than Tough (Witherspoon)	*My Little Baby* (Berns-Farrell)
Stormy Monday Blues (Walker)	*I Got A Woman* (Charles)
Baby What You Want Me To Do (Reed)	*Philosophy* (Morrison)
	Friday's Child (Morrison)

This is a 1977 release of nine Van Morrison and Them tracks from the mid-1960s. London Records packaged the songs quickly and there are minimal liner notes and a small drawing on the front cover. The highlight of this album is Jimmy Page's excellent guitar work, and the inclusion of a number of hard to find songs. Among these are "Philosophy," "Friday's Child," and "The Story Of Them, Parts 1 and 2." What is interesting about the album is that Van has always maintained that Them was simply an Irish pub band which played its best music at the Maritime Hotel in Belfast. He implied that the group Them no longer existed once it left Northern Ireland.

For Van Morrison collectors the lure of this album is the inclusion of blues tunes like "Baby What You Want Me To Do" and "Bright Lights, Big City." The magnificent manner in which Van is able to interpret the blues is one of his strongest attractions for American fans. There is also hint of early British rock and roll influences and a smattering of psychedelic musical influences which dominated American music from 1966 to 1968. While the album does not have any of Van Morrison's personal production touches, nevertheless, the quality of the music is outstanding.

SIDE ONE HIGHLIGHTS In a seven minute and 28 second song, "The Story Of Them, Parts 1 and 2," Van provides some rare autobiographical insights into the problems faced by Them in early tours of Germany, England, Ireland and America. Using images of conservative businessmen, moral hypocrisy and the crowds' frenetic desire for raw rock and roll music, Van paints an honest picture of the struggle that rock musicians experienced in the early 1960s. "The Story Of Them" has Dylanesque lyrics, and Van beautifully portrays the degree of alienation felt by many young people. As Greil Marcus has suggested, rock and roll "was a waiting game." While Van was stuck in Germany performing cover tunes for bored G.I.'s during the early 1960s, the Beatles were in Hamburg, the Golliwogs—soon to be known as Creedence Clearwater Revival—were playing in battles of the bands with Peter Wheat and the Breadmen in San Francisco, and Jerry Miller and Don Stevenson of the Moby Grape were playing with the Frantics in Seattle. Once the rock and roll revolution emerged in the mid-1960s, these artists would find varying degrees of fame and fortune. However, at this time they as well as Van were experiencing the frustrations of the rock revolution which was almost half a decade away. Van captured and capsulized these feelings in "The Story Of Them." The three blues tunes which follow, "Times Getting Tougher Than Tough," "Stormy Monday Blues," and "Baby What You Want Me To Do" are excellent examples of Van's blues roots.

SIDE TWO HIGHLIGHTS Jimmy Reed's "Bright Lights, Big City" is another superb blues song by Van. "Philosophy" and "Friday's Child" are two early and very rare Them cuts and they are a nice contrast to the blues tunes. There is a decided Yardbirds tinge to these songs, and the vocal stylings owe a great deal to Mick Jagger. The majority of the songs on this album were recorded in mono and only "My Little Baby" and "I Got A Woman" are stereo songs. Unfortunately, the rest of the tunes were reprocessed in stereo by London Records.

SUMMARY This album was released in an attempt to exploit Van's growing popularity in America. If London Records had bothered to provide adequate liner notes and a more attractive cover photo this album would have increased its sales. The music is excellent but it is an album for the hard-core Van Morrison collector.

A PERIOD OF TRANSITION (1977)
WARNER BROTHERS BS 2987

SIDE ONE
You Gotta Make It Through The
    World (Morrison)
It Fills You Up (Morrison)
The Eternal Kansas City
    (Morrison)

SIDE TWO
Joyous Sound (Morrison)
Flamingos Fly (Morrison)
Heavy Connection (Morrison)
Cold Wind In August (Morrison)

A Period of Transition celebrated Van's return to recording after a three year lay-off. The decided New Orleans flavor of Van's songs is enhanced by the presence of Mac Rebennack (Dr. John). This is straight ahead music which would make Professor Longhair, Huey Smith or Bobby Marchan grin with approval. Dr. John co-produced the album with Van, and the result is some of the most commercial music from Van Morrison in the late 1970s.

SIDE ONE HIGHLIGHTS "You Gotta Make It Through The World" has a bluesy quality as does "It Fills You Up." Both songs bear the unmistakable horn arrangements characterized in Dr. John's music. A mystical choir opens "The Eternal Kansas City" and for a moment the listener feels as though he or she is in a church. Then an almost jump arrangement makes "The Eternal Kansas City" an excellent rhythm and blues influenced song.

SIDE TWO HIGHLIGHTS The good-time music of the early 1970s is reflected in the opening number of side two. "Joyous Sound" is a tune which is reminiscent of the *Moondance* or *Tupelo Honey* albums. Although "Flamingos Fly" was a Top 40 type song, its release during the midst of disco mania was the reason for its lack of commercial success. "Heavy Connection" is a blues-oriented number which is used to evoke images of the "reefer man." "Cold Wind In August" is the last song on the album, and it is another blues-inspired song with a strong story line.

SUMMARY This album is for Van Morrison die-hards and fans of New Orleans music. It has some of Van's more commercial rock music from the late 1970s, but the album did not sell very well. None of the songs made the *Billboard* charts and there is a redundant feel to the music which may have hurt the album's sales. Still, it is an excellent piece of work.

WAVELENGTH (1978) WARNER BROTHERS BSK 3212

SIDE ONE	SIDE TWO
Kingdom Hall (Morrison)	*Wavelength* (Morrison)
Checkin' It Out (Morrison)	*Santa Fe / Beautiful Obsession*
Natalia (Morrison)	(Morrison-DeShannon)/(Morrison)
Venice U.S.A. (Morrison)	*Hungry For Your Love* (Morrison)
Lifetimes (Morrison)	*Take It Where You Find It*
	(Morrison)

Wavelength is an excellent commercial rock and roll album. A seven piece backup band augmented by Van's saxes, electric piano, acoustic guitar, and acoustic rhythm guitar makes up the bulk of the music. The Band's Garth Hudson accompanies Van on two songs with an accordian, Yamaha synthesizer and organ. When the album was produced Van agreed to tour for the first time in four years to promote its sales. Although Van had played numerous northern California clubs, he had not toured extensively since 1974. Lester Bangs' review in *Rolling Stone* succinctly summed up the album: "It makes a lovely sound, breaks no rules and keeps its grimy snout...out of the dark places..."

SIDE ONE HIGHLIGHTS "Kingdom Hall" is an autobiographical piece about Van's visits to the Marin County Jehovah's Witness Kingdom Hall. It is an unusual song since Jehovah's Witnesses do not have choirs present in their services. Perhaps this song is an allegorical comparison between a local Kingdom Hall and one of Van's favorite small concert halls, the Inn of the Beginning in Cotati, California. The next song uses mediation as a means of bringing two people together. "Checkin' It Out" is an attempt to suggest that any means of reuniting close friends is important in relationships.

"Natalia" was written for a close personal friend who helped Van through a period of personal crisis. It has a bluesy touch and Van effectively uses images of the summer to intensify the song. "Venice U.S.A." is a song which was written while Van was in southern California recording for Warner Brothers. He visited the small bohemian town of Venice and reflected on its beauty and sense of freedom. The song has a strong feeling augmented by intense lyrics. The final song, "Lifetimes," is a personal look at the music in Van's soul. He contemplates a lifetime of music and romantically suggests it will be with one special person.

SIDE TWO HIGHLIGHTS "Wavelength" was the only chart song from the album, and it appeared for 11 weeks on the *Billboard Hot 100*. Although it only rose to number 42, nevertheless, it was the song which reestablished Van's hit-making abilities. Peter Barden's synthesizer is particularly effective on this song. In "Wavelength" Van whimsically recalls his first AM hit, "Brown-Eyed Girl," by suggesting: "Won't you play that song again for me, About my lover, my lover in the grass." "Santa Fe" and "Beautiful Obsession" are performed as one lengthy tune. The former was co-written with Jackie DeShannon and it is a poignant tune about someone returning to Santa Fe, New Mexico after a failed romance. "Beautiful Obsession" is a song with a mystical western quality.

"Hungry For Your Love" was featured in the 1982 movie, "An Officer and a Gentleman," and it is the perfect tune to capture the essence of someone searching for romantic love. The album ends with "Take It Where You Find It" which is a plaintive plea to find a purpose in life. Most of the songs on this side reflect a strong commitment to finding some new meaning in a world dominated by crass commercialism, war, and a generally unhealthy lifestyle. Van is a voice of reason crying out in the wilderness.

SUMMARY To appreciate this album it must be played over and over again. There is a depth in the lyrics and a musical quality which is not apparent immediately to the listener. Some of Van's best songs are included in this album, and the music is a blend of blues and good-time rock and roll.

INTO THE MUSIC (1979) WARNER BROTHERS HS 3390

SIDE ONE
Bright Side Of The Road
  (Morrison)
Full Force Gale (Morrison)
Stepping Out Queen (Morrison)
Troubadours (Morrison)
Rolling Hills (Morrison)
You Make Me Feel So Free
  (Morrison)

SIDE TWO
Angeliou (Morrison)
And The Healing Has Begun
  (Morrison)
It's All In The Game
  (Dawes-Sigman)
*You Know What They're Writing
  About* (Morrison)

This album introduced two of Van Morrison's most accomplished musicians, reed players Pee Wee Ellis and Mark Isham. They helped to develop Van's interest in horns, and this has given a musical direction to Van's songs reminiscent of the *Moondance* album. Brief appearances by Robin Williamson, Ry Cooder and Zakir Hussain provide some interesting musical interludes.

SIDE ONE HIGHLIGHTS The uptempo "Bright Side Of The Road" leads off the album. This is one of Van's happiest songs and Katie Kissoon's backup vocals are outstanding. This is a joyful song suggesting positive changes in Van's life. "Full Force Gale" is an unusual tune for Van as he speaks of being "lifted up again by the Lord." It is a beautifully written song about his rededication to Christian values. Ry Cooder's slide guitar is an excellent contrast in this musical arrangement.

"Stepping Out Queen" is another happy but shallow song which is simply a tale of a young girl getting ready for a good time. Perhaps Van is intoning someone he knows to simply look at him as a person. "Troubadours" is lyrically and musically a folk song augmented by Robin Williamson's entertaining penny whistle background. The horn section moves in behind Van to underscore the meaning of the song. "Troubadours" suggests that song poets may be the only people able to use a "freedom song" to entertain the average person.

"Rolling Hills" reflects the style of an Irish brogue and it suggests that Van's religious faith and song writing skills were foremost in his life. "You Make Me Feel So Free" is an uptempo song about the new sense of freedom in Van's life.

SIDE TWO HIGHLIGHTS This side begins with "Angeliou" which is an autobiographical tale about Van's travels in Paris. Despite its modern theme there is an almost antiquated folk music tone to the song, but this simply underscores the seriousness of the lyrics. "And The Healing Has

Begun" is a unique song which evokes images of love, religion and companionship. When Van speaks of the healing of the soul, he uses the line, "When you hear the music ringin' in your soul, And you feel it in your heart and it grows and grows." The healing is rock and roll music. The next song, "It's All In The Game," is the old 1950s classic made famous by Tommy Edwards. This classic ballad provides a new forum for Van Morrison's talents, and he displays an unusual sensitivity in his version of "It's All In The Game."

"You Know What They're Writing About" is a love song which elaborates the theme that love is a healing process, but along the way there are a number of obstacles. The four songs on side two may be the most romantic section in any Van Morrison album. As usual the lyrics are complex, enigmatic and intriguing, and they provide rare glimpses into Van's feelings and sense of compassion.

SUMMARY This is a unique album because it combines straight ahead rock and roll music with strong feelings about love, life and the world. It is a curious mix of songs and ideas, and it may be Van's best work since the early 1970s. "Bright Side Of The Road" appeared briefly for one week in the 110 position of the *Billboard* 45 chart.

LIVE AT THE ROXY (1979)
WARNER BROTHERS WBMS 102

SIDE ONE

Brown-Eyed Girl (Morrison)
Wavelength (Morrison)
And It Stoned Me (Morrison)
Checkin' It Out (Morrison)
Hungry For Your Love (Morrison)
Kingdom Hall (Morrison)

SIDE TWO

Crazy Love (Morrison)
    (vocal by Katie Kissoon)
Tupelo Honey (Morrison)
Caravan (Morrison)
Cypress Avenue (Morrison)

Live At The Roxy is a promotional record issued only to radio stations. Warner Brothers arranged a concert at Hollywood's premier rock emporium, The Roxy, in an attempt to garner increased air play. This album was sent to radio stations on January 19, 1979 to promote Van's *Wavelength* tour. The Roxy album is a solid hour of some of Van Morrison's best music. It has been bootlegged but the originals are very difficult to purchase. The album was mailed in a red cover with "Live" in black and white letters at the top left corner and "The Warner Bros. Music Show" listed as the title on the bottom of the album cover. This album turns up in used record bins, and I am surprised that Warner Brothers has not issued it as a live concert album. This album was recorded in a November 26, 1978 concert held for a specially invited audience.

SIDE ONE HIGHLIGHTS   The announcer intones "George Ivan Morrison," and Van leads off with a rousing version of "Brown-Eyed Girl." To promote his tour, "Wavelength" is Van's next song. It is a raw, emotional version of the album's title song, and this leads into "And It Stoned Me" from the *Moondance* album. The next three songs are from the *Wavelength* album, and they display Van's extraordinary ability to mesmerize an audience.

SIDE TWO HIGHLIGHTS   Katie Kissoon opens this side singing Van's "Crazy Love," and this is followed by versions of "Tupelo Honey," "Caravan," and "Cypress Avenue." These live performances are equal if not superior to the album, *It's Too Late To Stop Now.*

SUMMARY   This is a rare opportunity to listen to an hour of Van Morrison in concert just before he embarked on a lengthy North American tour to promote the *Wavelength* album. This quality piece of Morrison's work is a must for all serious collectors.

COMMON ONE (1980)   WARNER BROTHERS BSK 3462

SIDE ONE	SIDE TWO
Haunts of Ancient Peace (Morrison)	*Wild Honey* (Morrison)
Summertime In England (Morrison)	*Spirit* (Morrison)
Satisfied (Morrison)	*When Heart Is Open* (Morrison)

When *Rolling Stone* magazine reviewed *Common One* they stated that "Van Morrison tries for heaven but can't forget hell." This is a misinterpretation of Van's musical direction and lifestyle in the 1980s. It is often difficult for rock critics to view a creative songwriter as anything more than an artist with a tormented soul. In contrast to the critics, Van has settled into a dull, somewhat mundane life in Marin County and this explains why his recent song writing reflects love, religion and tranquility. Unfortunately, this does not square with the hip New York rock critics' view of life. This album is about living in a rural setting and enjoying life. Tom Carson of *Rolling Stone* suggests that Van's "acceptance of orthodox Christianity can't help but reduce him in scale." C.S. Lewis would smile at this inane statement since it suggests that some rock critics believe that only certain subjects are necessary in rock lyrics.

SIDE ONE HIGHLIGHTS   "Haunts Of Ancient Peace" was recorded from February 11 through February 19, 1980 at the Super Bear Studios in the south of France, and the song generally reflects the rustic French countryside. "Summertime In England" is a therapeutic song in which Van recalls his European travels in the late 1970s. "Did you ever hear about Wordsworth and Coleridge?" Van asks. "They were smokin' up in Kendal." This song about British writers and poets is an allegorical suggestion that the "Common One" is art. Van always viewed himself as an artist first and a musician second, and this album reaffirms that fact. This side concludes with "Satisfied" which is a simple love song about walking "up that mountainside." The band provides an excellent vocal backup, and the songs on this side display a new depth in Van's song writing.

SIDE TWO HIGHLIGHTS   "Wild Honey" has a cocktail lounge musical tone but the lyrical beauty of Van's composition makes it an effective love-oriented tune. The next song, "Spirit," is one which articulates strong inner feelings, and it reaffirms the necessity to maintain a spirit in the face of adversity. The final song, "When Heart Is Open," has a cathedral music tone and is a mystical and haunting song pleading for compassion.

SUMMARY   *Common One* is a beautiful album lyrically and musically but the music is not commercially directed. There is a renaissance feeling in the lyrics, and the pleas for love, compassion and understanding are the album's focal points.

BEAUTIFUL VISION (1982)
WARNER BROTHERS BSK 3652

SIDE ONE	SIDE TWO
Celtic Ray (Morrison)	*Cleaning Windows* (Morrison)
Northern Muse (Solid Ground) (Morrison)	*Vanlose Stairway* (Morrison)
Dweller On The Threshold (Morrison-Murphy)	*Aryan Mist* (Morrison-Murphy)
Beautiful Vision (Morrison)	*Across The Bridge Where Angels Dwell* (Morrison)
She Gives Me Religion (Morrison)	*Scandinavia* (Morrison)

Beautiful Vision is largely in the same mold as *Common One*. There are, however, some excellent new additions to Van's band. Chris Michie's guitar work is an outstanding part of the album and Marin County legend John Allair contributes some melodic solos on the organ. Mark Knopfler of Dire Straits adds some excellent guitar solos on "Cleaning Windows" and "Aryan Mist."

SIDE ONE HIGHLIGHTS   The use of pipes in the opening song, "Celtic Ray," is an unusual and effective means of establishing the mystical European qualities of this album. In "Celtic Ray" Van yearns for Ireland and talks about his loneliness in America. "England and Wales I hear the voices calling," Van intones as he nostagically recalls his youth. "Nothern Muse (Solid Ground)" is a difficult song to interpret because it is obtuse and vague. The search for love, stability and direction in life are its common themes. The next two songs, "Dweller On The Threshold" and "Beautiful Vision" extend this theme. "She Gives Me Religion" emphasizes the important shifts in Van Morrison's life. It is a perfect tune to conclude this side of the album.

SIDE TWO HIGHLIGHTS   "Cleaning Windows" is the most autobiographical song on the album. Van fondly recalls his Belfast youth spent cleaning windows and playing the saxophone on weekends. It is surprising that Warner Brothers did not promote "Cleaning Windows" as a 45, because it generated a response similar to "Domino" in Van's 1982 concerts. "Cleaning Windows" is interesting because of its references to Sonny Terry, Muddy Waters, and Jack Kerouac. This tune offers revealing insight into Van's character.

   "Vanlose Stairway" is another song which is virtually impossible to interpret, but it is probably part of Van's search for peace and contentment. "Aryan Mist" is an allegorical look at confusion in modern life and it is a more sophisticated version of the spiritual music that Bob Dylan has composed in the late 1970s and early 1980s. This theme is carried on in "Across The Bridge Where Angels Dwell" as Van looks into a new life "where angels dwell." The final song, "Scandinavia," is the finest instrumental song written and recorded in Van's twenty year musical career. It is an interesting way to end a sensitive album.

SUMMARY   *Beautiful Vision* is strictly for Van Morrison die-hards who care about love, relationships and the future. "Cleaning Windows" is the only song with commercial air play potential. Yet this album is one of Van's strongest personal statements on his life in the early 1980s.

ONE MORE TIME: THEM FEATURING VAN MORRISON (1982)   DECCA 9286 900 (Netherlands)

SIDE ONE	SIDE TWO
Here Comes The Night (Berns)	*Richard Cory* (Simon)
I Put A Spell On You (Hawkins)	*Philosophy* (Morrison)
Baby Please Don't Go (Williams)	*One More Time* (Morrison)
All For Myself (Morrison)	*Don't Start Crying Now*
Don't Look Back (Hooker)	(Moore-West)
How Long Baby (Gillon)	*One Two Brown Eyes* (Morrison)
	Half As Much (It Won't Hurt) (Berns)

This is an English Decca release manufactured in the Netherlands. It includes twelve of Van's blues and rhythm and blues numbers. The inclusion of early original compositions such as "Philosophy" make this a unique album. The picture on the front cover shows Them in 1965 in a maudlin pose. The packaging is excellent and the music is outstanding. This is the type of rerelease which indicates the Europeans are light years ahead of the American record industry.

SIDE ONE HIGHLIGHTS   Bert Berns' "Here Comes The Night" and Van's "All For Myself" are the songs which demonstrate why Van Morrison was such an incredibly popular artist in the mid-1960s. John Lee Hooker's "Don't Look Back" is vintage Van covering an American blues tune.

SIDE TWO HIGHLIGHTS   "Philosophy" is the most unique song on this side but "Don't Start Crying Now" is a must for early Them fans. Although many of these songs are available on other releases, it is still an impressive album.

SUMMARY   This is a nicely packaged European reissue of early Van Morrison and Them. There are no liner notes, but the beautiful front picture is worth the price of the album.

THIS IS WHERE I CAME IN - VAN MORRISON (1982) BANG RECORDS 6467625

SIDE ONE

Spanish Rose (Morrison)
Goodbye Baby (Baby Goodbye)
(Berns-Farrell)
He Ain't Give You None (Morrison)
Beside You (Morrison)
Madame George (Morrison)
T.B. Sheets (Morrison)

SIDE TWO

Brown-Eyed Girl (Morrison)
Send Your Mind (Morrison)
The Smile You Smile (Morrison)
The Back Room (Morrison)
Ro Ro Rosey (Morrison)
Who Drove The Red Sports Car
(Morrison)
It's All Right (Morrison)
Joe Harper Saturday Morning
(Morrison)
Midnight Special (arranged by
Bert Berns)

This is an English repackaging on the Bang Record label. It is a fine early Van Morrison package because it includes fourteen of his best Bang tracks. The cover is beautifully designed with a picture of Van entering a taxi cab in New York City. Although it is a drawing of young Van, nevertheless it fits perfectly into the theme: "This Is Where I Came In." By featuring so many of his best early solo tunes, Bang has reissued a package which makes up for all its previous sins.

SIDE ONE HIGHLIGHTS   The two best songs on this side are "Madame George" and "T.B. Sheets." All of the cuts on this side appeared on previous Bang albums and this compilation does not utilize alternate cuts or different mixes of any songs.

SIDE TWO HIGHLIGHTS   This side contains nine songs and uses the same versions of the songs which appeared on earlier Bang albums. What is significant about this side is the inclusion of story-oriented blues songs like "The Back Room."

SUMMARY   This is a nice repackaging of Van Morrison materials from his Bang Record days. The album carefully notes the year of each song, and the over-all production is excellent. If you plan to purchase a Van Morrison album from his Bang Record days, this is the one to buy.

THEM FEATURING VAN MORRISON (1982)
DECCA TAB 45

SIDE ONE

Gloria (Morrison)
The Story Of Them (Morrison)
Stormy Monday (Walker)
Mystic Eyes (Morrison)
Hey Girl (Morrison)
Baby Please Don't Go (Williams)

SIDE TWO

Here Comes The Night (Berns)
My Lonely Sad Eyes (Morrison)
Richard Cory (Simon)
(It Won't Hurt) Half As Much ★
    (Berns)
Turn On Your Lovelight
    (Malone-Scott)
I Put A Spell On You (Hawkins)
Don't Look Back (Hooker)

★ *Note that the title of this song is different on One More Time, a 1982 Decca album manufactured in the Netherlands.*

In 1982 Decca Records in London repackaged a number of early Them songs. The liner notes by Roger St. Pierre are the finest to appear on any Van Morrison album. The thirteen tunes were carefully selected to represent the best of Van's early material, and the liner notes provide a capsule history of Van Morrison and Them which explains more than most in-depth magazine articles. The classic picture of Van Morrison and Them on the album cover suggests that the English do a much better job than Americans of repackaging their rock and roll legends.

SIDE ONE HIGHLIGHTS The first four songs are familiar Van Morrison numbers. The surprise on this side is "My Girl" which was written by Van but not released on the early American albums. It is a slow ballad with romantic lyrics. There is also a side to Van's early career virtually ignored by the English record companies and this is Van's penchant for obscure blues songs. By including Big Joe Williams' classic "Baby Please Don't Go" Decca Records has provided an important insight into Van's early musical development. The intensity and emotion behind "Baby Please Don't Go" helped it rise to number eight on the U.K. pop charts in January, 1965. It was typical of the energy of early Van Morrison.

SIDE TWO HIGHLIGHTS After the classic "Here Comes The Night" Van launches into "My Lonely Sad Eyes" from the *Them Again* album. This is followed by Paul Simon's "Richard Cory" which English Parrot released as an English 45. Van's version of "Richard Cory" is a unique interpretation of a folk tune. It is another example of the tremendous range of Van

Morrison's talents. The remainder of this side includes some of Van's classic early blues tunes and they are a delight.

SUMMARY   This is a fine compilation of Van Morrison's talents. It includes early Them songs as well as a number of blues tunes not common to Van's early American albums. The liner notes and excellent picture on the front cover make this 1982 release an excellent one. This album is a must for all serious Van Morrison collectors.

INARTICULATE SPEECH OF THE HEART
(1983) WARNER BROTHERS 1-23802 *(to be released in March, 1983)*

SIDE ONE
Higher Than The World
(Morrison)
Connswater (Morrison)
River Of Time (Morrison)
Celtic Swing (Morrison)
Rave On, John Donne (Morrison)

SIDE TWO
*Inarticulate Speech Of The Heart
No. 1* (Morrison)
Irish Heartbeat (Morrison)
The Street Only Knew Your Name
(Morrison)
Cry For Home (Morrison)
*Inarticulate Speech Of The Heart
No. 2* (Morrison)
September Night (Morrison)

This album was not available for a listening preview at the time of publication. However, Warner Brothers graciously provided an analysis of its content. *Inarticulate Speech of the Heart* contains five instrumental songs which develop jazz and folk music themes. Like many of Van's recent albums there is an eclectic quality to this work. This latest album is the product of weaving together many familiar themes of Van's past music. One of these is his Irish heritage which is evident in at least six songs. There is also a rhythm and blues tone to the song "The Street Only Knew Your Name." This song was one that Van had performed publicly for years and shows his continued interest in R and B music. It was originally recorded in 1975 for an album. (See the center section of the book for trivia listings for more information.) Van's writing shows new direction and skillful integrating of music and lyrics which has pushed his creative efforts to a new high.

The *Inarticulate Speech of the Heart* album is another indication that Van Morrison's musical genius continues to develop and explore new ground. He works hard at a type of music which avoids predictable cliches and formula writing. In 1983 Van will perform a number of live dates in England in March and plans a tour of Ireland for the summer. David Hayes was the assistant producer on this album and Van handled all the songwriting and the majority of the production work. The band has continued to be much the same as it was on each album since *Into The Music*. The guitar work by Chris Michie remains an outstanding part of the band and contributions from Mark Isham, Pee Wee Ellis, Peter Van Hooke and John Allair help to form the nucleus of Van Morrison's sound in the mid-1980s. This is obviously Van's best band and one hopes that he will continue to record and tour with this group.

Van during a promotional tour for *A Period of Transition*, 1978.

About the Author

Howard A. DeWitt is a Professor of History and Popular Culture at Ohlone College in Fremont, California. For almost two decades he has taught courses in history and popular culture. He is a widely published scholar with eight books on varying subjects. In the field of rock music his publications include *Chuck Berry: Rock N Roll Music* (1981) and *Jailhouse Rock: The Bootleg Records of Elvis Presley*, written with Lee Cotten (1983). Pierian Press will publish a second edition of the Chuck Berry book in 1983.

After completing his Ph.D. in American Studies at the University of Arizona in 1971, DeWitt taught at Cochise College, Chabot College, and the University of California at Davis. His musical experience was gained in the late 1950s when he was a promoter in Seattle, Washington and presented such acts as The Wailers, Little Bill and The Bluenotes, The Frantics, and Ron Holden and The Playboys.

He is presently at work on a study of The Yardbirds and has completed a manuscript on Elvis Presley's early life entitled *Sun Elvis*. In 1983 he toured Europe lecturing on the career of Chuck Berry.

Other Books by Howard A. DeWitt

Popular Culture

Chuck Berry: Rock N Roll Music (Horizon Books, 1981)
Jailhouse Rock: The Bootleg Records of Elvis Presley,
 with Lee Cotten (Pierian Press, 1983)

History and Government

California Civilization (Kendall Hunt, 1979)
Readings in California Civilization: Interpretative Issues
 (Kendall Hunt, 1981)
In the Course of Human Events: American Government,
 with Alan Kirshner (Kendall Hunt, 1983)

Ethnic Studies

Images of Ethnic and Radical Violence in California
 Politics, 1917-1930: A Survey
 (R and E Research Associates, 1975)
Anti-Filipino Movements in California.
 (R and E Research Associate, 1976)
Violence in the Fields: California Filipino Farm Labor
 Unionization During the Great Depression
 (Century 21 Publishing Company, 1980)

Contributors

Lee Cotten is the owner of Golden Oldies, 809 K Street Mall, Sacramento, California, 95814. He provided the 45 records, many of the albums, and the selected memorabilia used in producing this book. Lee's store is a mecca for the serious record collector. He also co-authored *Jailhouse Rock*, a study of the bootleg records of Elvis Presley, with me. I am indebted to Lee for his counsel, friendship and in-depth intellectual knowledge of rock and roll history.

Bruce A. Nichols and Larry Ray are record collectors and musicians. They live in the Detroit area and work for *Goldmine* magazine. Bruce and Larry provided much of the material in section two of the book, and the discography is largely their work. Bruce was also an excellent critic on sections one and three of the book and I would like to thank him for his strong input in the book.

Jeff Hughson is director of the American Music Archives and he also operates a collectors mail order record service, American Music Company, P.O. Box 19143, Sacramento, California, 95819. Jeff deals in new, used, and rare records. For his catalog send $1 or 3 IRC's to the above address. I gratefully acknowledge the aid of his Van Morrison Archive Collection in the completion of the book. Also, many of the rare records needed for this study were found through the American Music Company.

Dennis Loren is a Detroit area graphic artist. He is responsible for the cover design. In addition to consulting on a wide variety of graphics projects, Dennis is the design editor for *Goldmine* magazine. He also has designed 100 record sleeves for 45s and LPs.

Vinita Chhugani is a well-known San Francisco rock artist. She received her formal training at Ohlone College and she has a wide variety of rock and roll sketches. Her drawings of Van Morrison and her sketch of Jim Morrison are just a few examples of her excellent rock and roll tapestries. Her drawings may be purchased through Horizon Books for $10 each. For a list of Vinita's drawings send a self-addressed stamped envelope to Horizon Books.